OPERA ANTICS
&
ANECDOTES

From Amy on May 29, 2006

SOUND AND VISION

OPERA ANTICS
&
ANECDOTES

STEPHEN B. TANNER

SOUND AND VISION

*Laughter and Music are the best antidotes
for gloom in the world — or closer to home*

CONTENTS

FOREWORD

SAMUEL JOHNSON CALLED OPERA "an exotic and irrational entertainment"— and at least he got the second part right.

I mean, what's rational about an art form in which some Mimi in a massive muumuu is supposed to be wasting away to nothing, an art form where tiny tenors romance strapping sopranos and all the singers convey their secret emotions and innermost thoughts at full blast to the seats in the very back of the hall?

Still, without opera we would be deprived of so much beautiful music, and besides, a lot of people would be out of work, standing on street corners wanting handouts or, worse, singing in subways for spare change. And, as Stephen Tanner points out in this entertaining expanded second edition, without opera we'd be deprived of a raft of fine, funny and very amusing stories about singers, managers, impresarios and others who make up the strange and wonderful world of the opera stage.

Going around in diplomatic circles has given Tanner enviable access to opera people around the world, not only as an audience member, but also as someone who's carried a spear, not to mention a tune or two. [My own biggest experience with full-scale opera came as child in the Coro dei Ragazzi, or "ragamuffin chorus," in a production of *Pagliacci*. At least I got to be dressed up in rags as a peasant boy, unlike one of my fellow choirboys — now a world-famous baritone in the big leagues, so I won't embarrass him by mentioning his name — who got stuck wearing the only costume left over, as a peasant girl. Still, it doesn't seem to have warped him nor hurt his career.]

In his travels over the years, Tanner kept his eyes and ears open, gathering up all sorts of fascinating and amusing stories. [If you find him standing next to you at intermission, you should be careful what you say. He might just write it down.] Some of Tanner's best tales come not just from the musicians themselves but also from stagehands, chauffeurs and other behind-the-scenes folks who really know the score and know, as it were, where all the bodies are buried.

But for all that he jokes about its pomposity or silliness, it's clear that Tanner really does love opera, as only someone who knows it well truly can. Underlying the entertainment and amusement, there's a real sense of affection that helps temper his tales of temper tantrums and overblown egos.

If opera seems tedious, *Opera Antics & Anecdotes* demonstrates that if you were aware of all the deliciously funny goings-on behind the curtain, you would never again consider opera boring.

David W. Barber

PREFACE

OPERA PEOPLE LAUGH AND TEASE A GOOD DEAL. With a bit of mirth they can thumb their noses at each other — and at lesser frustrations. Their laughter centres on the eternal *leitmotifs* of theatre life: idiocy, vanity, flubs, mishaps, putdowns, "numskul-duggery," and of course sex.

Earthy *irreverence* backstage is in ludicrous contrast with the hushed *reverence* on the audience side of the curtain.

I have roamed the opera galaxy for over 60 years, sharing laughter and friendship not just with a few stars, but also with conductors, savants of the claque, stage directors, masters of the glockenspiel, scenery designers, ticket scalpers, voice gurus, balcony wits, critics, singers' agents, ushers, opera historians, throat doctors, fellow voice students plus buffs and fanatics of every sort. Almost all had something droll and down-to-earth to say about this oh-so-serious, lofty art.

Most operas are sexist, racist and politically very incorrect, what with plots glorifying male-dominated societies run by elit-ist gods, funky aristocrats, and all manner of egomaniacs bent on war, murder, rape, incest, kidnapping, torture, and every imaginable treachery and intrigue. Traditionally, in these 19th-century melodramas the soprano loves the wrong guy, disobeys the male who is bossing her around — daddy, brother or guard-ian — and ends up in a nunnery, insane or suicidal. The moral lesson to young ladies in the audience is not subtle.

Of course, opera plots distort reality, but backstage humor, like a funhouse mirror, does a much more thorough job of it: tenors are dimwitted meatballs, sopranos are fatuous fatsos, and conductors are sexist, stilletto-tongued bullies, whereas rival singers are scheming, over-the-hill screech owls and foghorns. Artistic directors, critics, singers' agents, or anyone higher than you in the backstage pecking order are half-wits, charlatans and hacks. So backstage palaver is chock-full of tales about blowing adversaries and higher-ups clean out of the water. Aside from humbling enemies and bigwigs, items that tickle opera people most are about things that looked, sounded or went wrong. Things that went right aren't funny. A fine performance will be talked about for weeks, but an birdbrained blunder may be laughed at for decades.

My goal is to preserve in print some rare glimpses of opera people and pungent theatre life viewed through a prism of humor. It is not my wish to poke fun at opera, which I love, or at specific persons or organizations — though that is precisely what opera folk themselves often do [out of earshot of the public, of course].

A word of caution before we begin: opera yarns usually ring true as humor, but often not as history. There are at least three reasons why: first, opera folk add, embellish and dramatize when they tell stories; second, some yarns — such as the allegation that Australian soprano Nellie Melba used fresh semen to keep her vocal cords young and pliant — were doubtlessly concocted and spread by enemy forces; third, opera performers remember punchlines, but muddle up or forget completely the who-where-when details. [This drives historians and researchers mad.] Stories, such as the one about gigantic basso Luigi Lablache trying to pass himself off as a midget or the old chestnut about Lohengrin missing his swanboat, exist in three or more wildly different versions. They can't all be correct. Which ones are? Who knows?

When all is said and done, opera people deserve far more credit than they get. Except for members of a bomb-disposal squad, few humans work under such stress, not knowing what may go wrong in the next minute or so — or, worse, what to do about it when it happens.

Almost all opera pros who reach the top went through fiercely competitive apprenticeships, full of sacrifices and very hard work. Hats off to their dedication and artistry. Thanks also for their dazzling and entertaining displays of the glorious cussedness of human nature.

But enough! *Allons-y! Fanget-an!* Get on with it! Maestro, the Overture, please!

Stephen B. Tanner

Chapter 1

Overture Capricciosa

Opera people are at their best either retired and in their anecdotage, or eating, drinking and blowing off steam after a performance.

Looking back to many after-opera eating and drinking bouts, I see my opera pals crowding into some Italian restaurant, ravenous and parched. Waiters rush to arrange a longer table. The local theatre manager offers the conductor the head chair. "No, no, that honor belongs to you as general manager." So, the conductor ends up wedged between the soprano and the tenor. Spouses and hangers-on shuffle towards the foot, wine appears from nowhere, and jibes about idiocy, fluffs, and the other quaint motifs of theatre life begin to fly.

A German bass starts off, "Once there was a tenor so stupid that even other tenors began to notice."

"How would you know?" an Italian tenor wisecracks, "You may have enough voice for three basses, but you haven't enough brains for half a tenor. [Laughter.] But have you heard about the Canadian prima donna who boasted she'd insured her voice for two million bucks? 'Oh,' purred her rival, 'how did you use the money?' "

11

When the laughter dies, some one else pipes up, "In *Traviata*, the soprano was paying zero attention to Toscanini's baton and held her high notes till the tenor needed a shave. So, fuming like a volcano ready to blow, Toscanini sent her his card at intermission. He had to speak to her. When he came into her dressing room, she was sure he wanted to compliment her on her great singing, so she held out a fat paw for him to kiss. He just shoved it aside, grabbed and shook her queen-size breastworks, and hissed, "If only these were BRAINS!"

By dessert, the laughter and "quippervescent" repartee are deafening. Around 2:00 a.m. the conductor raps his glass and proposes a mock toast: "I think, before any of you offers to pay the bill, we should drink to my wise old Viennese mentor, Franz Schalk, who said 'every theatre is a nuthouse, but an opera theatre is the ward for the incurables.'"

Some pay their share and dart for the door. Others stay on, standing in knots and in no hurry to stop their teasing pleasantries and go to bed. They too finally dwindle out the door and sober up a bit walking in the fresh night air. No one plans to get up before noon. [Incidentally, I have never heard a singer at table bad mouth another, unless the other had just gone home or to the toilet.]

Was Schalk being facetious? Or are opera theatres nuthouses and wards for the incurable? Was Schalk hemi-semi-demi-on target? You decide.

Chapter 2

Mishaps, Flubs, Ad Libs — And General Havoc

"Hey there, watch what you're doing!"

AIR RAIDS BOMBED MANY A GERMAN THEATRE to bits during the last Great War. Rebuilt in 1951, the Frankfurt Opera had the largest revolving stage in all Germany. It was over 30 meters in diameter. Every avant-garde stage director yearned to explore its vertiginous possibilities.

The director of a *Don Giovanni* had a brainstorm. Why not have the Commendatore astride a live white horse in the opening park scene and then, at the very end of the opera, turn the stage and show the park scene and the equestrian statue again?

This idea required maneuvering the Commendatore in the dark. Split-second teamwork was required. Two stage assistants rehearsed over and over again, escorting the Commendatore in his heavy costume and shoving him up onto the nag.

On opening night, the park scene with the Commendatore on his white steed drew a terrific hand, but when the final scene came, things fell apart. First, the stagehands couldn't find the horse. Next a stirrup strap broke. The basso was rushed around to the other side of the equine and hoisted astride, but as he reached out for the reins, the lights went up, and ...

•

One hour before curtain time the 230-pound soprano for *Norma* cancelled. Her slim, trim sub was hurriedly escorted to the makeup and costume departments, where it turned out her costume had vanished. The only costume available was that of the 230-pounder designed by Omar the Tentmaker. It was six sizes too large and particularly baggy in the chest area. Since needle and thread and safety pins couldn't do the chest job, the costume lady shouted at the sub, "Go as fast as you can up to the prop room and ask for prop number 77, shove it down the top of your dress, and scamper back here as fast as you can. It's curtain time in ten minutes."

Minutes later, the soprano was back, out of breath and looking very unhappy, a large piece of sponge rubber stuck out of her dress, bulging up under her chin. "Oh, my God!" screamed the costume lady, "I said prop 77, not 79! That's Falstaff's behind."

•

In the very first Alaskan production of *Carmen*, staged in Anchorage in 1965, Elizabeth Mannion sang the title role. A local sled dog musher was her Don Jose and the head backstage technician was an Inuit, a very dear man. Now, in the last act this tech was to raise the stage level for the scene when Carmen is killed, but on opening night the flustered tech pushed the wrong button. The stage abruptly sank. Net result: Carmen disappeared to all except those in the upper balcony and all Carmen could see of the conductor was, now and then, the tip of his baton.

•

Florence Foster Jenkins had a voice hard to do justice to in mere words. If other wobbly sopranos have had pitch problems, how would you describe hers? There have been socialite screech owls before and after her, but none matched Jenkins. Her recordings are incomparable, especially her rendition of the Queen of the Night's Aria. Thanks to a railroad she allegedely iherited, she was able to rent Carnegie Hall for annual recitals, and since she chose pieces hysterically beyond her talents, her presentations were the rage among concertgoers with love for the ridiculous.

One day Jenkins was shaken up in a rather bad Manhattan taxi collision, but instead of a rebuke, the driver received a box of fine Cuban cigars with a thank-you note: "Thanks to the accident you had, my dear man, my high-C is higher than ever before."

•

Giacomo Lauri-Volpi, the tenor with very dramatic high notes, had a curtain problem in *Trovatore* in Rome. Brandishing his sword, he hit a clarion high-C on the words, "*All 'armi*," but the fast curtain closed him off. Furious, he wrenched the curtains apart and stuck his head and sword arm out, still trumpeting that big high-C.

Tenor Giuseppe Venditelli had a similar problem at that very point in *Trovatore*. Waving his sword high, the curtain plummeted down, knocked off his wig and ruined the tenor's most glorious moment in the opera.

•

Virginia Ferni Germano had an hourglass figure, but most of the sand had sunk to the bottom. In *Carmen* at the Costanzi Theatre in Rome she had her back to the audience as the curtain closed at the end of Act III. As luck would have it, she was too near the footlights and the curtain draped fetchingly around her widest beam. The public guffawed. When she learned why her posterior had become "a butt of wit," she was so mortified she locked herself in her dressing room for half an hour before they could coax her out again.

•

At Covent Garden in about 1959, Arturo Sergi was singing Max, the tenor lead in an English-language version of *Der Freischütz*. Covent Garden had a penchant for using original props and weapons wherever possible. So the rifle firing the magic bullets was an old muzzle-loading carbine complete with flints. It made a terrible BANG whenever Sergi fired it in rehearsal, but for some reason at dress rehearsal when shooting down the eagle in the first act, the darned thing went POOF instead of BANG. Sticking to the libretto, Sergi as Max had the following exchange with James Pease singing the part of Kaspar:

Max: "What sort of bullet was that?"

Kaspar: "You know very well."

Max: "Do you have another one just like it?"

The rehearsal collapsed as conductor Rudolf Kempe, the orchestra, and cast tried to stop laughing.

•

In the early 1990s a German company was rehearsing *Der Freischütz*. They had reached the next-to-last scene when the evil Kaspar is mortally wounded by a magic bullet. Kaspar curses both heaven and the devil and then falls dead like a ton of bricks. When this particular bass hit the deck, he let out a loud, hideous fart. The chorus' next line was, "That was his dying prayer."

In 1928 in the Po Valley town of Faenza, a tenor from Oklahoma, Joseph Horace Benton — better known on stage as Giuseppe Bentonelli — made a memorable debut in *Faust*. In the garden scene when Joe leapt up onto a window flower box and reached out to hug Marguerite, his tights, as if on cue, cascaded down around his ankles. The vision of his suddenly tightless behind brought down the house.

Naturally, news of the event spread like wildfire in the press and via the opera buff grapevine. Ribbing backstage was merciless, but Benton had the benefit of free publicity. He became an overnight matinée idol sought after by impresarios and agencies. The public flocked to see and hear the handsome young man who dropped his drawers in Faenza.

•

A more titillating case of southern exposure hit tenor Luigi Ottolini while singing Radames in Lisbon in the 1960's. In the second act the costume covering Radames's midsection was simply a pair of black jockey shorts. As Luigi came on stage carried by slaves and sitting on a throne-like chair, Giulietta Simionato as Amneris, and the bass singing the King, cracked up when they noticed Luigi's open fly with his most intimate part dangling.

Similarly, Lawrence Tibbett's trousers split up the back as he leaned forward to lift a fallen soprano. Also, in *A Masked Ball* while singing the line, "I'll see her again in ecstasy," Richard Tucker's belt busted and his pants obeyed the law of gravity.

Female costume contretemps usually involve split seams or falling underwear, particularly the long pantaloon type worn in many 19th-century operas.

Eugenia Burzio as Santuzza in *Cavalleria Rusticana* felt her long underdrawers slipping slowly down toward her ankles. Without bending over or missing a note, she stepped out of them and gave them a deft kick toward the prompter. And WHOOSH! They ended up wrapped around his face.

•

World famous as Carmen, Emma Calvé was prancing and singing a lively *Seguidilla* when her waistband broke and her long drawers cascaded to the stage. Freeing herself from them, she jauntily flipped them to the chorus members behind her, who proceeded to tug and toss them back and forth with glee.

•

The beauteous Marcella Pobbe gave her audience an eye-catching thrill when Otello shoved her to the floor so roughly that her low-cut gown slid even lower and her pulchritudinous breasts popped out for all to admire.

•

What about ad libs?

In a *Rigoletto* produced by Boris Goldovsky, young Sherrill Milnes was singing the title role in English. Nearing the end of Rigoletto's monologue, *Pari siamo*, instead of, "it is an evil omen; ah, no; it's madness," Sherrill blew it and sang, "It is an oval eeman." Then, realizing his fluff, he ad-libbed, "ah, no! It's a round one."

•

When the orchestra was badly out of synch in the last duet of *Trovatore*, tenor Aureliano Pertile got even: instead of singing, "Ah, this damned woman sold her love!" [*Ah, quest' infame l'amore venduto!*], he ad-libbed, "Ah, this damned, sold-out orchestra!" [*Ah, quest' infame orchestra venduta!*]

•

A young American bass bet his friends he could sing the words "rotten eggs" instead of "Radames" in the trial scene of *Aida*. He did and was sacked.

•

In Chicago, Fyodor Chaliapin was singing *Boris Godunov*. He knew almost none of the spectators understood Russian, so he ad-libbed to his manservant in the wings, "Get the whiskey bottle out; this opera's almost finished."

•

In *Die Fledermaus* Beverly Sills was wearing a very low-cut evening gown and while throwing her and the tipsy tenor in jail, Frosch the jailer took a long, unrehearsed look down her cleavage and explained in a stage whisper to the audience, "Hmmm, king size!" After the laughter subsided, he lurched over for a second deep look and commented, "And with filter tips."

In some theatres by the time guest artists arrive, the opera in question has been in rehearsal — or even in performance — but some guests and last-minute subs get only a piano rehearsal at the most. So, they step out unfamiliar with the stage sets, the acting routines, and their colleagues. As a result …

A soprano singing Amelia in *Ballo in maschera* had never seen the sets, so she came on stage in the third act through the fireplace instead of the door.

•

Also in *A Masked Ball,* a last-minute guest baritone in Stuttgart had no earthly idea what costume or mask the tenor was wearing in the final scene's ball, so he stabbed a masked chorister instead of Riccardo.

•

In Germany in the last act of whatever opera it was, the baritone pulled the trigger, but no shot rang out. The tenor clutched his breast and ad-libbed, "Your stare is killing me." Then "BANG" came the truant pistol shot. So, the tenor gasped in noble agony, "And on top of all the rest, that TOO!"

•

In another opera when the shot did not ring out, the baritone kicked the tenor smartly in the rear with his boot. As the tenor collapsed to the stage, he sang out, "That boot was poisoned." [*Der Stiefel war vergiftet*]

•

Again in *Tosca* in Germany, baritone Günter Reich once substituted as Scarpia at the very last minute with no time at all for a stage rehearsal. It was a very nerve-racking and tiring evening. So, when he finally lay dead at Tosca's feet, he was relieved and exhausted. As he lay there eyes closed and half asleep, the soprano placed a cross on his chest. Thinking this was the signal that the scene was over, he rose to his feet with his back to the footlights. Suddenly he noticed a horrified look on Tosca's face and heard murmurs of surprise from the auditorium. — Oh, oh! What to do? Turning to the public, he made a slow, deep bow — and strode to the wings at a brisk clip.

•

During *Pagliacci,* baritone Angelo Pilotto's mind went blank. A panicked look at the prompter elicited two words, "Walk slowly." So Pilotto began trudging slowly. Again the prompter said, "*Cammin adagio.*" Pilotto shrugged and continued until OOOPS! It dawned on him that he was supposed to SING "Walk Slowly." By this time the conductor, the orchestra and public were convulsed, since in true Italian style, the audience knew every word in the opera.

•

Another communication failure between stage and prompter involved Robert Merrill who loved to tell about the time he was singing Figaro in *Barber of Seville*. Suddenly, he couldn't remember what came next and glanced desperately toward the prompter's box at the footlights, but the prompter had his eyes closed and wore a silly grin. Merrill, left in the lurch, had to fake it for a few bars.

At intermission, the young prompter confessed that his girl friend had made him lose all sense of reality by administering an impromptu Monica Lewinsky treatment.

•

In Northern Germany many repertory theatres put on both opera and plays. A young prose theatre actor and opera chorus member had just been fired, but the management asked him to stick around for that evening's *Lohengrin*. Miffed and with nothing to lose, he decided he would be a chorus knight the audience would never forget. So, while Lohengrin was singing his first aria, he took out a roll, broke it, and started feeding Lohengrin's swan.

Parsifal was in rehearsal in a southern Spanish city. After all, the Temple of Monsalvat in that opera was supposed to be in Spain, wasn't it? In any event, the lead singers and the stage director were imported Germans, whereas the choristers and minor singers sang in Spanish.

When the punctilious German stage director finally arrived, he was unnerved to find preparations were a hornets' nest of confusion and far behind schedule. Coming to grips with this mess, he had to work at a snail's pace through an interpreter. Then to top it all, the chorus of Knights failed to appear for dress rehearsal. In such disjointed turmoil, our hassled stage director could find no time until 24 hours before opening night to tell the Knights of the Holy Grail how to behave during the Good Friday scene.

"Now, after your entrance, array yourselves about two meters apart along this white line I've drawn on the stage. Then on the fourth measure of your music, cross your arms and place your hands on your chests like this. After that I want you ..."

The interpreter interrupted, "Maestro, hum it for them."

"What on earth do you mean? Don't they read music?"

"Well no, Maestro — but don't worry, they know their parts. Just hum it for them."

"Good Lord! I've never run into such a situation. How can I teach them to read music between now and tomorrow night? What are we going to do? ... Wait! I have it. It's the only way: tell them I'll stand in the wings; they must watch me; I'll act their parts and all they have to do is do what I do."

After the translation, the choristers nodded to show they understood.

"Well," thought the stage director, "it could be worse. Now I can devote the little time left to ten other problems."

Opening night all was going smoothly. The Knights crossed their arms on cue and aped the director's poses and gestures. Then all of a sudden, the tenor singing Parsifal emitted a cringe-worthy high note that sounded like ripping canvas. The director

put his hands to his mouth in shame. The chorus did likewise. The audience exploded in laughter. The director, now in shock, yelled *"NEIN! NEIN!"* and signaled the chorus to cut it out. The chorus signaled the audience to cut it out and said *"NEIN, NEIN!"* More howls of laughter. Completely out of control, the director started swearing and signaled vigorously for the chorus to cease and desist. The chorus imitated his words and gestures to a roar of guffaws and horselaughs. On the verge of nervous collapse, the director saw the only way to stop them gesturing was to disappear. So he walked back out of sight, at which point the chorus obediently trooped off stage.

Chapter 3

Other Lands, Other Customs

ONE FROSTY DECEMBER NEW YORK morning in 1909, baritone Enrico Pignataro stepped elatedly off his ship from Naples, clutching his Manhattan Opera contract. In the cab to his hotel, his elation changed to cold terror: there were Christmas wreaths on almost every door! Back in Naples, a wreath on the front door meant one thing only: a recent death at that abode. Enrico dashed off a letter home as soon as he reached his hotel: "I have arrived safely, but a plague has hit this city. People are dying like flies. There are wreaths on almost every door. Light many candles for me in church and pray that I may leave this place alive."

•

New York scared the wits out of Arturo Toscanini, also with a funeral wreath. While the myopic Maestro was taking a footlight bow, a fan laid a wreath at his feet. In Italy this type of wreath was meant only for funerals or graveyards. It took a few seconds before Toscanini saw what he was holding. Recoiling, he hurled the accursed flowers away and dashed off stage very flustered. Friends told him it was just an innocent gaffe, but Arturo was rock sure some enemy was telling him to drop dead.

•

According to Russian conductor Juri Aronowitsch, when an Italian prima donna addressed the stage director at the Bolshoi as "Madam Director," the Russian replied haughtily, "It is not *Madam*, it is *Comrade* Director."

While saying farewell, the Italian soprano told the Comrade Director she was bound for Genoa to sing a Puccini opera. "Oh, which?" inquired the Russian.

"*COMRADE Butterfly*," she smirked.

•

24

Also at the Bolshoi, in the early 1970s, a striking red-headed American soprano received a standing ovation at her debut. A Soviet government minister appeared at her dressing room door after the show with flowers, compliments, and an invitation to share a cozy champagne-and-caviar supper with him.

Sensing the chance to strike a blow for freedom, she said she would be delighted to sup with him but on one condition — that Jews and anyone else wishing to leave the U.S.S.R. be allowed to do so.

"Aha," said the Russian, "from this I understand you wish we should be completely alone."

•

A stellar Italian troupe came to Berlin in the early 1930s and included two top spinto/drammatico tenors of the era, Giacomo Lauri-Volpi and Aureliano Pertile, who were not only at the top of their form, but also pretty much unrivaled for brassy, wild-animal high notes. At a gala banquet, Signora Pertile was seated next to a bemonocled Prussian stuffed shirt who clinked glasses with her early in the meal and confided to her, "We are so glad your husband came; we can't stand that Pertile." [Unfortunately, the anecdote omits what happened after he found out he was talking to Pertile's wife.]

Many singers feel mournful and homesick when they have to spend a month or more living in foreign lands, crashing into language barriers. Basso Tancredi Pasero said his case was typical. Asked why he had spent only five seasons at the Metropolitan, he replied, "I was too homesick for Italy and my friends. While I was in New York I only went to Italian restaurants and played scopa and other card games. All my free hours were spent with other Italians. So, naturally, I never learned much

English at all. But then, Giulio Gatti-Casazza, the general manager at the Metropolitan, seemed to have only one sentence in English which he used whenever possible. It was, 'ThenKK you, eVVV-ree-BAW-dee.'"

•

Russian basso Fyodor Chaliapin knew some Italian and French, but almost no German the first time he came to Berlin. In the train, he acquired some wild ideas about population control in Germany: at every station he saw printed on toilet doors in large capital letters, "ABORT." [toilet] "Abort" in Russian means "abortion."

•

Like Chaliapin, Richard Tucker misinterpreted a foreign word when he made his Italian debut at the Arena di Verona in 1947. The opera was *La Gioconda*, with Maria Callas also making her Italian debut. After Enzo's big aria, the audience went wild and clamored for an encore, shouting "Bis! Bis! Bis!" Though he had been studying Italian opera for over ten years, this was a new word for him. Tucker turned excited and perplexed, and asked his coach, Paul Althouse, "What's going on? Why are they calling me a BEAST?"

•

An up-and-coming Russian soprano gave a recital in New York. Before the reception in her honor at the Russian consulate general, she asked the Consul what was the proper thing to say when shaking guests' hands in the reception line.

"Just say, 'I am so delighted,' " he replied.

So, beaming at each guest she cooed, "I yam so-o-o delightful!"

•

Another fine artist with peccable English, but impeccable manners, was the Spanish basso Count Andres de Segurola. At a white-tie-and-tails Metropolitan Opera banquet in honor of the attractive Australian soprano Frances Alda, he stood up in high fettle to toast her, saying, "Alda, permit me to say a few words on your behind." [He was a true gentleman and had no bass — I mean base — intentions.]

•

Back in the 1970s when he was still learning American slang, Luciano Pavarotti is credited with saying, "I theenk she ees wat you call in English 'a pushunder.' "

•

At a reception in England, a French soprano was asked what her husband did. "He ees a pubic-relations expert for a beeg industry." [That's certainly transforming public into private relations.]

•

Baritone Tittá Ruffo laughingly recalled a dinner with Enrico Caruso in August 1915 when they were at the Colon Opera in Buenos Aires to do *Pagliacci*. The pair went out for dinner together in the city's most sedate Italian restaurant. During the main course, a loud marital squabble erupted at the next table. Suddenly, the husband slapped his wife hard across the face with the back of his hand. Caruso winced. A few minutes later, the churl hauled off and swatted her again. Caruso was so upset that he jumped from his chair, napkin in hand, and gave the fellow a tongue-lashing about ungentlemanly behavior. At this point, the lady in question hauled off and smacked Caruso across the chops as hard as she could and told him to mind his own damned business. Holding his cheek and gaping with amazement, Caruso retreated to his own table and sulked for the rest of the meal.

•

In Detroit around 1945, Bulgarian baritone Ivan Petrov was invited to sing for the Greeks of that city. Since most of the music would be in five-four time, he needed local help to find an accompanist. During the concert the young lady chosen did an excellent job at the piano. Petrov was elated and wanted to express his thanks. So, he beamed and said, "I like you. You feel me good."

Two immigrant gentlemen from a small East European town had just arrived to live in New York. The year was 1926. They started out on their first Saturday afternoon to get acquainted with the city and its customs.

They stopped outside a shop where a large sign in the window mystified them. It said "MANICURE."

"You go in and find out what that means. I'll wait here," said the first fellow.

"Well?" asked the first fellow when his pal finally re-emerged.

"I paid one dollar and a lady cut my fingernails. So now we know."

One block further, they passed another shop with a mysterious sign: "PEDICURE." "Now," said the second guy, "it's your turn and I'll do the waiting."

After about 20 minutes, he came out and said, "I paid a dollar and a half and they cut my toenails. So now we know."

Strolling further, they saw on the Metropolitan Opera marquee the perplexing word, *"WALKÜRE."*

"It's your turn again," said the first man.

His friend came back in a flash and said excitedly, "I didn't wait to find out what they do in there. They wanted ten dollars just for a ticket. Who knows what they cut for ten dollars!"

•

In the early 1950s, an elated Michigan couple told their local travel agent they were about to fulfill their lifelong dream: "to hear and see Wagner's *Lohengrin* at the Bayroot Festival." The agency briskly arranged air and ground reservations.

An on-the-spot photographer fed German wire services a photo of two fit-to-be-tied Michiganders at the airport in Beirut, Lebanon, brandishing tickets for *Lohengrin* the next evening in Bayreuth, Germany.

These misdirected Midwesterners were not alone. Wagner himself in 1876 ordered the dragon for *Siegfried* from a London firm. The finished monster was so bulky, he had to be boxed in two crates. His front half went to Bayreuth, but his rear end

— you guessed it — came to the perplexed, wide-eyed attention of Syrian customs officers dockside in Beirut. Was this some insulting infidel trick?

Germany 1934

While living in Germany, the author noted that to show intense enjoyment of classical music, many Germans either shut their eyes and knit their brows or else stare fixedly at a point in the air some three feet in front of their noses.

Chapter 4

And You Call That Acting?!?

A COUPLE OF CENTURIES AGO, opera singers stood stock-still on stage, but their relative positions told everything. An old bore poet/librettist, Pietro Metastasio, put it this way: "If the more illustrious character stands on stage left and the lowlier on the right, they can be distinguished in various ways, for example locating the former a few steps in front of the latter, or placing him center stage facing the audience, and the other far from him and further upstage, sideways to the public and facing his superior."

Acting has changed and grown a bit more vigorous since Metastasio's day, but country to country and era to era, huge gaps separate what passes for good acting or bad.

Rexford Harrower was a young American stage director with experience on both sides of the Atlantic when he applied for a job to old general manager Raoul Gunsbourg in Monte Carlo. Gunsbourg's response was, "We have never felt the need for a stage director to date, we do not need one now, and I do not foresee any need for one in the future."

At La Fenice in Venice where Harrower tried again, he was told "When we do German operas we have a German stage director; for Italian operas we have an Italian director; when we do French operas we have a French director. When we do an American opera, we will use an American director." Europeans say that Americans are good at producing planes, space vehicles, computers and automobiles, but not operas. [*Porgy and Bess* seems to be the only American work staged internationally with any regularity.] Harrower was later called to Venice to direct *The Jumping Frog of Calaveras County*, an American opera composed by Lukas Foss, a German. It was a success.

•

Mario del Monaco joked how hard it was to satisfy acting tastes in every country where he sang. In *Otello*, for instance, he had to act three different death scenes, depending on where he was.

"In Italy, I stab myself, stumble around, sink to the floor and then, with superhuman effort, I struggle up onto the bed, kiss Desdemona and slither slowly down for the long count. Now, in New York that won't do. In America when you're down, you're down, and you don't get up. So in America I stab myself, fall on the bed and later sink slowly to the floor on Otello's final notes. But at the Colon in Buenos Aires, where they pay me twice as much as I get in New York or Italy — I die twice."

•

In Naples in the war winter of 1943-44, *Lucia di Lammermoor* was staged at the San Carlo Opera to honor a Scottish division on leave from the front. The idea boomeranged. I was there.

The theatre was packed with boisterous Scots. When the curtains parted, they saw a cluster of short, swarthy, Neapolitan choristers in kilts, who were strutting about and waving their arms in broad Mediterranean gestures. This was Scotland? First chortles, then catcalls, and then bedlam broke loose. The music could hardly be heard.

That was just the beginning. Lucia looked too plump to be a Scottish lassie. More chortles and comments. But when the tenor appeared, he brought down the house. He was skinny as a broomstick and short. While he sang toward the audience about his vehement love for Lucia, she stood behind him, hands under chin, swaying like a forlorn sea lion. Mating advice in thick Scottish brogue filled the air. The first act finally ended despite occasional pandemonium.

The audience dwindled at intermission to about 30 souls. Perhaps those who left thought the rest of the show could never top that first act. They were right.

•

Not so long ago, opera acting was little more than concertizing in costume.

At a press conference in the 1930s, a Latin tenor was asked about acting. "Acting? Ha! Nothing to it. When I sing in the middle register, I raise the right arm. When I sing in the upper register, I raise my left arm. And when I hit a big high note, I raise both arms. Acting is no big deal." A few years later at a performance of *Aida*, a critic noticed this same tenor had changed his acting style. The critic asked the tenor, "How come in *Aida* you raised only your left arm?" "My right arm's for *Trovatore*," he replied.

•

Another famous "arm actor" was Giuseppe Fancelli (1833-87). This jolly, fat Florentine ex-stevedore had such glorious tenor high notes that Verdi cast him as Radames for the Italian premiere of *Aida*, even though Fancelli was musically illiterate and couldn't act. For Fancelli, "acting" meant stretching and waving both hands out in front of his chest with fingers spread. This earned him the nickname "Five-and-five-makes-ten."

•

Critic Ernest Newman in England penned the final word on "arm acting." "When an opera character raises one arm we are to understand that something or other has moved him deeply; when he raises both arms, his soul has been shaken to its foundations."

"The typical Wagnerian soprano looks like an ox, she moves like a cart horse, she stands like a haystack."

— Ernest Newman

•

Mark Twain on acting in Wagnerian operas: "As a rule, all you could see would be a couple of people, one of them standing still, and the other catching flies."

•

After the tenor in *Rigoletto* walked through the chorus to the rear of the stage, the stage director gave him hell. "But that's what Caruso always did," objected the tenor. Since Caruso's valet was still alive, the director phoned him and found out that, yes indeed, Caruso usually walked upstage at that point to clear his throat and spit.

•

Gaspare Spontini's opera *La Vestale* is about the vestal virgins. When, however, the stage director said, "I want all the virgins to move left to the far side of the stage," no one budged. So he changed it. "Would all of you *impersonating* virgins please move left." Everyone moved.

•

Les Troyens of Berlioz is another opera with vestal virgins. Russian-born Boris Goldovsky staged its American premiere at the old Boston Opera House in March 1955.

In the opera, the Trojan vestal virgins choose suicide rather than face rape and slaughter at the hands of Greek invaders. However, in rehearsal there weren't enough rubber daggers to go around, leaving half a dozen virgins with no way to kill themselves. The chorus director, Sarah Caldwell [then unknown outside Boston,] asked Goldovsky what to do. His impatient, whiny comeback was, "Zee rast weel dreenk poison from their rrrings."

•

Early in Richard Tucker's career, Toscanini stopped him abruptly after *O terra addio* during a piano rehearsal of *Aida* and casually asked, "Have you ever made love with a woman?"

"Maestro, I have a wife and children."

"Well, then SING as if you felt love," thundered Toscanini. "Make me feel this love."

•

Conductor Otto Klemperer had reached the point at a *Fidelio* rehearsal where Leonora unlocks the dungeon door to let her beloved Florestan out. Suddenly Klemperer yelled, "SCHTOP! SCHTOP!" Everything stopped.

Limping badly after a recent stroke, Otto slowly staggered down from the podium, stumbled his way through the door to backstage, then up the stairs, and over to Leonora. It took him all of five minutes while everyone waited to see what on earth he had in mind. He snatched the large key from the soprano's hand, put it in the prison door lock and started to turn it clockwise, saying, "It doesn't turn THIS WAY, but THE OTHER WAY!" He then tottered back to the podium and the rehearsal recommenced.

CHAPTER 5

AUDIENCES LOVE YOU TODAY
AND ASSASSINATE YOU TOMORROW

Italy 1946

WHAT DO OPERA STARS GENERALLY FEEL about their public? Some answers might read like this:

We in opera have very mixed, bittersweet feelings about audiences. On the sweet side, of course, is the high, the euphoria when fans roar approval. We need them. How could we earn a living if they didn't buy tickets and recordings? The bitter part is that they adore you today and kill you tomorrow — *and* they give standing ovations to your worst enemies. Our careers are too often in the hands of semi-cognoscenti and incognoscenti who clap and crow "bravo" for some big name voice in terminal decay. Yes, in our business, after you make a name for yourself you can pee in bed. Your fans will claim you merely sweated.

Caruso also knew name glamour was more important than voice and delighted in proving that most audiences couldn't tell one voice from another even if you paid them.

In March 1905 at Chicago, Caruso was on as Canio in *Pagliacci*. Versatile Met second tenor Albert Reiss was to sing Beppe and Arlecchino, but Albert had bad, bad laryngitis. What to do? Caruso came to the rescue. "Do not worry, Alberto, you make the words with your mouth and I sing Arlecchino's arietta for you." He even bet Albert the audience and the critics would never know the difference. He was right. He sang behind the scenery and Reiss mimed and mouthed the part out front. Result: zero applause. After all, why applaud second tenor Albert Reiss?

•

Caruso had fun proving his point again in his Manhattan apartment. He played some recordings of some third-rate Italian tenor and his socialite guests told him he had never sounded better and his renditions were magnificent.

•

Another tenor who loved to put one over on his listeners was the jolly Bohemian giant Leo Slezak. He tells in his memoirs that for small-town recitals in Germany and Austria, he would sometimes sing some Schumann or Schubert rarity and claim that his miniature, cross-eyed accompanist had composed it last week. After such numbers, he would modestly step back and let the little pianist take the applause.

Yes, opera people tend to find fault with audiences in every country — including their own. Though English himself, conductor Sir Thomas Beecham was wont to say, "The English don't like music, but they love the noise it makes." He also averred that English tenors were as sonorous as "yawning giraffes," whereas English sopranos sounded as if they "subsisted on a diet of seaweed."

•

Clara Louise Kellogg (1842–1916) was the first American prima donna to take London by storm. She might also be called a "prima damner." Here's what she had to say in her memoirs about London audiences:

"I believe from the bottom of my heart that, inherently and permanently, the English are an unmusical people. They do not like fire, nor passion, nor great moments in either life or art. Mozart's music, that runs peacefully and simply along, is precisely what suits them best. They adore it. They likewise adore Rossini and Händel. They think that the crashing emotional climaxes of the more advanced composers are extravagant; and, both by instinct and principle, they dislike the immoderate and the extreme in all things. They are in fact a simple and primitive people, temperamentally, actually, and artistically." Wow!

Around 1900 two bemonocled Prussian lieutenants bought tickets to Rossini's *Wilhelm Tell*, thinking it was an operetta with dancing girls. Though disappointed, they felt obliged to sit through it to the bitter end.

The next morning over coffee, fellow officers asked them what they had seen at the theatre. "Utter nonsense," said one. "A civilian shooting at fruit."

•

The Scots in the middle of World War II suffered a shortage of everything; food, manufactured goods, you name it. Thus it was smart when you saw a line in front of a store to jump in and then ask what rarity was for sale.

So, when a small-town housewife spotted an impressive line, she queued up as fast as she could. Very out of breath, she asked what the line was for.

"*Tales of Hoffmann*," came the reply.

"Oh," said she, "they'll make a nice soup."

•

Afternoons before an evening at the Met, James Cash Penney, the founder of J.C. Penney stores, would pester his womenfolk to get a move on. J. C. had an ingrown punctuality fetish; however, once family members were ensconced in their loge, he would calm down, stroke his hair and beard and nod to friends. Then, as soon as the curtain parted, he would doze off and sleep soundly until intermission.

.

In a Po Valley theatre in Italy a fellow in the back of the audience hooted a wicked comparison between the slim soprano onstage and her fatso rival. As fanatic fans for each diva were in the audience, a free-for-all fight broke out. The singers onstage were impressed and applauded the audience. What a bargain to have high drama on both sides of the curtain for the price of one ticket.

.

'Twas opening night for Verdi's *Stiffelio* at Parma in 1968. A spectator in the third row was mightily perplexed: why on earth did his neighbor have a frying pan in his lap? A long quizzical stare brought forth this explanation: "Confidentially, some of my pals in the balcony plan to pelt the singers and the conductor with stuff and I want to be ready. You never know. They may throw some eggs too!"

•

Violinist Jascha Heifetz's recital in a north midwestern city fell on the third day of a rip-roaring blizzard. His train was so late he had to don his white tie and tails on the train. He arrived at the concert hall cold, hungry and fifteen minutes late. An audience of about two dozen greeted him. After complimenting them for bravery, Heifetz said he was not really accustomed to making music for so small a gathering. "Wouldn't it be more appropriate if you all joined me for a good dinner down the block?"

At this point, a white-headed gent rose and said, "Just to hear you, my wife and I drove eighty miles through this terrible storm at risk of life and limb. So, before we go to any restaurant couldn't you at least sing a couple of arias?"

•

When someone proposed importing European chandeliers for a new opera house in the American far west, the mayor called it "a dang fool waste of money, 'cause no one in these parts would know how to play 'em."

•

An Italian baritone just back in Milan from London told his cronies that the British habit of following librettos was simply amazing. One evening he was to sing *Trovatore*, but that was switched at the last minute to *Rigoletto*. During the first act, he watched several front row listeners thumbing *Trovatore* librettos trying to find something to match what Rigoletto was up to on stage.

A wild story has it that the Met came down with "acute usheritis" when the ushers struck for higher pay just hours before opening night curtain. What to do? Panic calls to every corner of Gotham, but by 5:00 p.m. it was clear: absolutely no one in a tuxedo was available on such short notice except a couple of dozen bruisers from the Bar Bouncers Association.

Between 6:30 p.m and 7:30 p.m these muscle-bound giants were assigned their positions and feverishly rehearsed in their duties.

First nighter habitués and sons-of-habitués were startled by the ham-fisted hulks who grabbed their tickets and told them where to go.

When a fashionably late dame sailed past a ticket-taker, he growled, "Hey dare, lady, where's ya ticket?" Pretending not to hear, she sailed on. "Hey, lady, ya gotta have a ticket to get in here!"

"Ah, my dear man — I have a mezzanine box."

"Lady," the bruiser told her, "I don' care if ya got gold-plated tits, ya gotta have a ticket!"

•

After a performance, a celebrated European tenor was strolling in front of the marquee at the old Met. Typically, he had his throat muffled up in a huge wool scarf and wore a jaunty fuzzy fedora. A New York dowager walked up to him, tapped him limply on the sleeve and said, "Aren't you the tenor who sang here last night?"

"Yessa, Madam, I yam," said he, tipping his hat, waiting with a smile for the inevitable compliment.

"I can't find my chauffeur. You have a strong voice. His name is Andrew. Would you call him?"

•

At an after-recital reception, a self-important society matron congratulated the soprano and beseeched her to sing *Adele's Laughing Song* at her next concert.

"But I just sang it at the end of the first half of this afternoon's program," the artist protested.

"You did? I wish I'd known. It's one of my favorites."

There are many stories about the adventures and misadventures of spouses, backstage or out front, while their other half is on stage.

Mrs. Puccini and Mrs. Augusta Pinza belonged to that coterie of wives who knew other women found their VIP husbands ultra-magnetic. They also knew Puccini and Pinza were not shy of beautiful women. In fact, having Ezio Pinza sing *Don Giovanni* was flagrant type casting. It followed that neither wife trusted her husband out of her sight for more than ten minutes. So, both spent lots of time at rehearsals and performances. Their efforts to keep tabs on their husbands' social lives were topics of hilarity. One evening there was much laughter when hefty Augusta Pinza wedged herself into the stagedoor phone booth at the old Met and then couldn't get the darned folding door open. House firemen had to extricate her.

Peter Greenough, husband of Beverly Sills, was seated in the fourth row of the New York City Opera for the first night of Donizetti's *Roberto Devereux*. Beverly Sills received a standing ovation at the end of Act Two. He applauded, but a fan on the row behind him leaned over and said, "Aren't you Beverly Sills' husband? Why aren't you standing and screaming like everyone else here?"

Peter replied, "I'm her husband, yes — but I'm not her cheerleader."

•

Baritone Kari Nurmela, early in his career, was singing a new role in a German theatre and asked his wife to tape his performance from her tenth row seat. This theatre, as most others, prohibited tape recording. So she kept her little recorder hidden in the folds of her evening jacket on her lap. When Kari came on, so did the machine, but it blared out a taping of Kari's voice singing in another opera, because she had pushed only the PLAY button. To compound her chagrin, it took a moment or two of fumbling before she could find and punch the STOP button.

•

In another case, soprano Lynne Strow Piccolo asked her husband to turn on their tape recorder whenever she was on stage, but in the dark he got things bass-ackwards: he recorded only when she *wasn't* on stage.

•

In a 1986 *Otello* in Hartford, Connecticut, English superscript translations did not clarify what was going on: a technician put the superscript tape for Act Three on during Act Two. Why the audience was chortling during such a serious opera completely mystified the singers on stage.

Opera buffs love to collect intimate souvenirs of famous singers, the more intimate the better. Autographed programs, photos and recordings are trivial compared with, say, a lock of Adelina Patti's hair, a handkerchief Pavarotti used on national TV, or a cigar butt of Caruso's.

Nineteenth-century prima ballerina Fanny Essler had a very sexy charisma, thanks to exceptional grace of face, figure and movement.

In Milan once, a wild gaggle of young male fans forced their way into her hotel room just after she had checked out. They fought over her bedsheets. One lucky admirer brandished over his head the ultimate trophy: her chamber pot. In the ensuing melee, the sheets were ripped to shreds and the potty fell and was dashed to smithereens. Throughout Milan, however, the potty shards and sheet swatches became elite prizes — and macho conversation pieces.

•

Dupont Nemours, like several other industrial giants, had its own box at the Met, but Dupont's loge was in a prime location right next to the general manager's. It served to host important Dupont clients, VIPs and upper managers from Dupont's own hierarchy.

In the 1970s it suddenly dawned on everyone that one particular manager in the New York office had never been invited, since everyone agreed opera theatres, art museums and the like were not places he would enter of his own free will. Nevertheless, to keep him from feeling like an outcast, he was invited and, to everyone's surprise, he accepted.

Seated in front cheek-by-jowl with general manager Rudolf Bing's loge next door, he, like J. C. Penney, dozed off almost as soon as the curtains parted and was soon snoring vigorously. His Dupont colleague peered over at the general manager's box and was shocked to see that there, brushing elbows with Dupont's snorer, was Sir Rudolf himself, staring down his noble nose at the snorer. The Dupont official discreetly nudged his man back to reality and whispered to him, "You're sitting next to Bing." The snorer, only half awake, gave a loud response that turned all heads, including Sir Rudolf's: "BING WHO?"

•

A Hungarian soprano was delighted to give her autograph for a second time to a beaming stage door boy, but when he asked for a third , she wanted to know why so many. "Well," the boy smiled, "for three of yours I can get one of Renata Scotto."

•

The Crown Prince of Cambodia arrived in Paris in 1863 on a state visit, just as France was strengthening its foothold in Southeast Asia. At the Théâtre de l'Opéra, he attended Bizet's *Pearl Fishers*, seated in the imperial box next to Napoleon III, of France.

During the opera, his normally smiling face grew grimmer and grimmer. During applause at the final curtain, the French Emperor inquired which part of the opera His Highness had liked best. "The first" came the reply. Napoleon III graciously ordered the overture to be played over again, but no sooner had it begun than the Prince became agitated and yelped in frustration, "No! No! No! Not that. Before. Before. The first. The first."

The Cambodian Ambassador leaned over and explained that the Prince had particularly enjoyed the sounds of the orchestra tuning up — it reminded him so much of the music of his beloved homeland.

Chapter 6

Yells From The Balcony — Back Talk From The Stage

Several decades ago in Italy, a dull cast was plodding through Verdi's *Otello*. For a while the spell of the music and drama held balcony wits in check, but after the feckless tenor shouted for Desdemona to produce the missing hanky — "the handkerchief! the handkerchief! the handkerchief!" a voice erupted from the back of the theatre, "For God's sakes, blow your nose on your sleeve and get on with the show!"

A tidal wave of laughter almost stopped the show. Ushers fanned the house to find the shouter, and four scowling German tourists stalked out muttering about desecration of Temples of the Arts, lack of respect for Verdi and Shakespeare — and so on.

Germans and Italians are divided by more than the Alps. They disagree utterly about yelling from the balcony. Some uppercrust Italians agree with the Germans and feel embarrassed by the *vox populi* antics of their countrymen, but they are a minority. Italians appreciate a juicy verbal tomato hurled at an unsatisfactory singer or cast. In fact, some quick-witted balcony bellowers become hometown heroes — particularly in Parma, the current world capital of peanut gallery putdowns. Until very recently the *Gazzetta di Parma* printed the choicest audience quips the morning after every premiere. Opera buffs in Parma agree fully with Verdi's comment, "For the price of a ticket the audience buys the right to cheer or to jeer."

Before going on to catcalls, here's a cross-section of Italian views on yells from the balcony, followed by a résumé of German opinion:

When we Italians buy tickets, we rent the theatre, the singers, conductor, and orchestra — all of them. We're their employers. Our taxes and our tickets pay both for the theatre and for their salaries. THEY work for us and are paid to please US — not the other way around. If the performance is sloppy, it's our duty as patrons of the arts and employers to point out that the public is being swindled. We have to remind both performers and management that we can exist without them, but they cannot exist without us, the audience.

We're not only commentators and critics, but also educators and judges. Peering down from the top of the theatre, we know that many fat cats and foreigners in the best seats haven't the foggiest idea what they are hearing and seeing. How would they know if the tenor blew his lines? Or if the soprano took her big aria down a tone or two so she wouldn't scrog on a high note?

Why, without us around, the general manager and his cronies would fill the stage with their mistresses, and the orchestra pit with their cousins and other nonentities.

In Italy, we regulars up in the top balcony are frequently moved to tears and thunderous applause by a great performance, and unlike operagoers north of the Alps we don't hide what we like or dislike. Lots of Germans stare at their opera scores instead of the stage. They must be trying to find musical mistakes, but when they find one, do they say or yell anything? No, they just scowl. So why do they bother to follow the score? Some Germans claim yelling from the balcony is not sporting. Not sporting? Hell, it's the best sport in town!

•

Well, what about German opinion?

We Germans absolutely detest yells from the public, and we are disagreeing completely with those Italians. Already the children we are teaching that Great Art speaks to them — not they to Art. Near Great Art one must be silent and show great respect. ·

Only a dunderhead or hired ruffian would break the holy spell of Great Art with vulgar catcalls, witty or not. An opera theatre is A Temple of the Arts, A Shrine to Music. It is not the Roman Colosseum or a bullfighting arena!

In a Temple of the Arts, there must be respectful silence while the music is playing. While the conductor leads the sacred rites with his magic little wand, he is like a High Priest, and the audience must feel the mystic barrier beginning at his coat-tails, separating the reality from the enchanted world on stage. Nothing from the audience must cross that mystic gulf while the music is playing.

Yelling while the curtain is open is worse than farting during the sermon in church.

Garlic and wine are known to excite the imagination. Beer and schnapps have a calming effect.

A third-rate baritone was struggling through Rigoletto's *Pari siamo* monologue. When he sang the line, "That old man cursed me," someone on the dark side of the curtain mused aloud, "Probably was Verdi."

•

During *Carmen* at the Paris Opera, Micaela was meandering far off pitch. The public sighed in relief when she left the stage. Later, when she reappeared, following an offstage rifle shot, a balcony commentator groaned, "Shit! They missed her."

•

In Milan the audience was thankful that an awful evening of *Tosca* was nearly over. The tired tenor was making a hash of his final aria, *E lucevan le stelle*, and when he came to the line, "And I'm dying in despair," "And you're not the only one!" [*E non sei solo*] came a fast retort from the balcony.

•

In Florence *La Boheme*'s Rodolfo had just begun his aria, "Your tiny hand is frozen" *Che gelida manina*, when some wag cackled, "Hah! You should feel her feet!" [*Sentissi che piedi!*] Caruso once added a touch of realism as he began this aria by dreamily slipping into Geraldine Farrar's hand a piece of ice.

•

In Parma in January 1970, baritone Giampiero Mastromei singing *Rigoletto* seemed so unmoved by his daughter's kidnapping that one listener blurted out, "You'd think they'd nabbed his mother-in-law."

•

Also in Parma, a second-rate tenor in *La forza del destino* had just sung the words, "Life is hell for unhappy me. In vain I long for death," when a helpful voice advised him, "Throw yourself under a trolley car!"

•

In Saarbrücken, Germany, in 1966, a new dissonant opera, *Moll Flanders*, by Heinz Fanels, was drawing to a close. Spectators squirmed in their seats, but maintained Teutonic decorum. The final scene, however, with the five principals standing on pedestals and singing out, "And now we're all going to the graveyard," was too much for one sufferer, who rumbled for all to hear: "Take the general manager with you."

•

A miscast prima donna was screaming away as Norma in Milan's old Carcano Theatre back in the 1920s. In the last act, after the tenor, Abrate, had lamented, "Ah, Norma, too late I came to know you," a loud voice growled in thick Milanese dialect, "Me, too! If I'd known her sooner, I wouldn't have wasted three francs [sic] on this ticket."

•

A baritone with a wobbly, ugly voice stuck his face through the curtains at the beginning of *Pagliacci* to ask the public's permission to come on stage, "May I?" Back came a snort, "NO!"

•

In another *Pagliacci*, this time in Parma in December 1968, Tonio came out between a clothesline of sheets, instead of appearing between the curtains for his Prologue. This produced immediate balcony reactions: "Must be laundry day," and "Never saw so many sheets even in a Brigitte Bardot movie."

•

In *Aida* a runt of a tenor, an altogether unmilitary shrimp, strode out as Radames, commander-in-chief of the Egyptian armies. Before he could drop his jaw for Radames' first line, a dismal voice from the top of the theatre intoned, "Oh Lord! The war's already lost."

•

Another even runtier broomstick of a tenor in *Aida* with a doomsday blaring voice came on stage in Florence. When he pumped out Radames's first words, "If I were that warrior. If my dream would only come true," some one in the balcony cackled, "You could kiss your own you-know-what."

•

In 1922 tenor Ismaele Voltolini, singing Radames in Parma, had done a particularly sloppy job. So, when the high priest in the last act sang, "Radames! Radames! Radames! Proclaim your innocence," a patron piped up, "He can't possibly do that."

•

Again in *Aida*, when Amonasro stuns Radames in the Nile scene by revealing he is none other than Aida's papa, baritone Giangiacomo Guelfi really boomed out the words, "*Suo padre*," holding on to the "*pa*" in *padre* for an eternity. When he finished, some wag whined, "Who'd ya say?"

•

For most Italians, *Tannhäuser* is "far out" in at least three ways: far too few melodies, far too little action, and far, far too long. Spectators in Florence were either impatiently on edge or asleep by 1:00 a.m. when the Pilgrims Chorus finally shuffled on stage. "Everyone still alive down there?" came the solicitous query from the top of the theatre. Another voice chimed in, "Can't they march faster? Don't they know it's after one?"

•

In a Po Valley theatre before the First World War, as soon as the long-haired tenor in *Trovatore* had sung the words, "When a cry came from Heaven which said to me …" a voice roared from the second balcony, "Get a haircut."

•

A Carmen in Paris with a tiny voice could hardly be heard. When she came to the line, "I'm singing for myself," someone in the middle of the house cried out, "Try singing a bit for the rest of us."

•

In a small Po Valley opera house, a bleating tenor singing Vasco da Gama in *L'Africana* was worse than dreadful. In the prison scene of Act II, just as the soprano was about to waken him, a bored voice cautioned her, "Let sleeping dogs lie!"

"Dogs," by the way, is an epithet often applied in Italy to unsatisfactory singers. Baritone Mariano Stabile explained it this way: "They are called dogs, because dogs are the only other animal that can bark for hours without getting hoarse."

•

When both the tenor and soprano in *Tosca* turned out to be awful, a critic wrote, "Since when are dogs allowed in church?"

•

A race was on to see which singer in *Tannhäuser* could get hoarse faster. Suddenly, the soprano clutched her throat, came to the footlights and said, "I cannot sing anymore," — to which a philosophical voice in the audience replied, "That is true."

•

In a Milan *Cavalleria Rusticana*, Turiddu had just sung, "I'm going to go outdoors," when a thoughtful voice advised, "Grab some toilet paper!"

•

On the opening of Verdi's *Il Corsaro* in Parma in 1970 there were no comments at all from the balcony. When asked later why the silence from above, general manager Giuseppe Negri replied, "You mustn't forget, we haven't put on this opera in over 50 years. They simply don't know it. Come to the second performance. By then, they're all experts."

•

In his native Catania, Sicily, Giuseppe di Stefano took the high-B at the end of *Celeste Aida* softly, the way Verdi wanted it sung, instead of blaring it out as tenors usually do. Some in the audience jeered and whistled. Di Stefano went to the footlights and announced, "That's the way Verdi wrote it!" Back flew a balcony know-it-all's retort, "Verdi made a mistake."

At La Scala several decades ago, the two Wagnerian singers Hilda Konetzni and Günther Treptow were wading through *Die Walküre*. Both vocally and physically these two fine artists could be rated only as heavyweights — or super-heavyweights. La Konetzni unfortunately tripped on the dimly lit stage, and, while helping her to her feet, Treptow slipped and sprawled on top of her. They wallowed for a while trying to help each other up. Had they been Italians, audience bellowers might have torn the theatre apart with guffaws, whistles, and mating advice. They were foreigners, however, and since Italians find Wagner too heavy to laugh at, there was only respectful silence.

•

In *Ernani* at Florence, soprano Vera Amerighi Rutili had the part of Elvira. She was a veritable blimp. So, when she began her aria, "Ernani, whisk me away," a gallery nut couldn't resist: "Believe me, Signora, he'll have to make more than one trip."

•

When undersize tenors and baritones struggle to lift or lug pudgy sopranos, balcony wits get out the heavy artillery. Thus, while Rigoletto labored to lift the sack containing his chubby daughter Gilda, a friendly voice advised, "Try it in two loads."

By the next performance, the irate stage director thought he'd found a way to silence hecklers: Rigoletto would carry a bulging bag without Gilda inside and then the stage lights would dim out for a few seconds so two stagehands could replace it with another burlap bag with the chubby singer in it. The trouble was, when the hecklers saw Rigoletto heave the sack over his shoulder, one of them sneered, "Can't be her!"

•

The owner of Asti's Restaurant in New York, baritone Adolfo Mariani, loved to tell a yarn about Astolfi, a young longshoreman from La Spezia. Astolfi had a beautiful, natural bass voice and the local opera bigwigs decided to have him debut as Dr. Grenvil in *Traviata*. Astolfi, however, looked and felt quite awkward in his last-act costume. Longshoremen are not used to wearing top hats and gloves or to carrying a cane. The stage director had to rehearse his entrance over and over again: take off your hat and put it on the chair with the cane; now take off your gloves and put them in the hat and then walk over to the bed and feel Violetta's pulse.

On opening night, however, poor Astolfi was a bundle of nerves: he walked over to the dying Violetta and felt her pulse with his gloves and hat still on and the cane tucked under his arm. At this sight, some one hollered from the rear of the theatre, "That's no doctor! That's a veterinarian!"

•

During a small-town *Faust* performance in France, Mephistopheles stepped onto the stage trapdoor to sink back into hell. Unfortunately, his sword jammed the mechanism and stopped his descent with half of him still above ground. Up in the peanut gallery someone crowed, "Lookie there! Hell's so full there's not even room for the devil."

•

In Lyon, France a soprano was clutching now her chest, now her throat, trying to convey desperation. A balcony wit yelped, "Oh, throw up and get it over with."

•

In *La Gioconda* the soprano of the evening had almost lost her voice before she reached her big final scene aria. As soon as she gasped the fatal word, "*Suicidio!*" some wag yodeled, "Do it right away!"

•

At the Teatro Regio in Parma, *Tosca* was on, but the foreign conductor's tempi were so slow that one balcony critic moaned aloud, "This year he'll give us the first act and next year the second."

•

53

Tuscan baritone Arturo Romboli [what a great name for a baritone!] was singing Valentine in *Faust*. When Valentine is killed in Act Three, someone yelled, "You cowards, you've killed the only good one in the show!"

According to the general manager, a virtual mirror-image incident occurred in *Faust* at the San Carlo in 1909; the baritone singing Valentino was well below par and when he died, the public murmured and one person applauded. Suddenly another yelled, "Bravo, Valentino, dying is the best thing you've done tonight."

•

Eugenia Burzio's bosom was bigger than huge. So, when she finished her invitation to the tenor in *Loreley*, "Come rest on my breast," a male chauvinist pig piped up, "Madam, we can come in droves!"

At La Scala, the soprano in *Don Carlo* was having a bad night. She had just sung the tragic words of Queen Elizabeth's great last-act aria, "Carry to God's throne my tears," when someone commented, "Also Verdi's, my dear."

•

The audience chuckled when the heroine of *The Bartered Bride* waddled on stage, almost as wide as she was tall. Promptly, a balcony knave chortled, "They'd better throw in a big bonus if they expect any bids on HER!"

Now let's listen to some backtalk from the stage:

One evening at the Rome Opera, Fyodor Chaliapin was singing the title role in Boïto's *Mefistofele*, sporting only a loincloth. His extravagant acting, dense Russian accent and nude torso combined to irritate the Roman audience. When a loud, derisive whistle came from the gallery, Chaliapin came to the footlights, motioned for silence and, using a skill he perfected as a deckhand on the Volga River, he let out an ear-shattering whistle that practically blew the roof off the theatre. Then, shaking his fist toward the balcony, he bellowed, "If you're going to whistle, DO ...IT ... RIGHT!

•

During a *Norma* in Naples, the audience roared and whistled at the substitute tenor. Mario Armandi took it for a while, but, finally exasperated, he walked down to the footlights and said calmly: "Look, I know I'm not singing very well, but I've a contract for six performances. If you'll shut up, I'll leave town tomorrow and some other tenor can take over. ... But, if you want to go on jeering, I'll damn well sing all six. Take your choice."

The audience applauded Armandi's pluck and behaved well for the rest of the evening. His voice warmed up and he did stick around for the other five performances.

•

The tenor in *Rigoletto* was hooted mercilessly after his first-act aria. Stung, he rushed to the footlights and snarled, "You whistled me! Hah! Wait till you hear our baritone!"

•

In the 1930s, tenor Galliano Masini in *Tosca* was having a bad night. The audience started howling right in the middle of his first aria. Masini sang on, but boiling inside, he waited for a chance to get even.

In the second act his voice improved, and by the last act he was singing superbly. For his final aria the audience gave him an ovation and yelled for an encore. Still smarting from the insulting first-act hubbub, Masini refused even to acknowledge the applause, but when cries for an encore went on and on, he stepped out between the curtains, crooked an elbow, and, with a slicing motion of the other arm, gave the audience instead of an encore, the old Italian "up yours" gesture.

•

Lest you think Masini's gesture unique, let's go to Mexico City of 1952, where Maria Callas was having an off night also in *Tosca*. The audience gave ovations to tenor Di Stefano and baritone Paolo Silveri, but had scant applause for Callas. With her prima donna pride cut to the quick, she too gave the audience the old sign-language "up yours."

•

On another occasion, Galliano Masini was singing at the Italian spa town of Montecatini, famous for its rather laxative mineral waters. Again his voice went haywire. This time, however, when he felt the first hint of audience unrest, he ran forward pointing into his mouth, and cried, "What do you expect? I've been drinking your damned water!"

•

At La Scala a few years after the Second World War, tenor Giacomo Lauri-Volpi — also noted for "off nights"— provoked a storm of whistles and jeers. When the din subsided, he rushed forward to confront his tormentors and shouted, "We are NOT in a *trattoria*. We're at LA SCALA!" — to which a voice from the balcony thundered, "Well, SING as if you were at La Scala!"

•

Maestro Giovanni Fratini of Milano recalled an unfortunate *Traviata* he conducted in a small Po Valley theatre. The tenor's nerves gave way in the first act and he barely made it to intermission before becoming sick to his stomach. What to do? Cancel and refund the audience's money? Not on your life. A chorister piped up. He knew Alfredo's part. So up went the curtain, but as the volunteer floundered through Alfredo's second-act aria, pandemonium didn't rain — it poured. The chorister sang on to the end and then ran to the footlights and shouted, "Shut up, all of you! If you don't, I'll sing it again."

•

Conductors can also talk back. In Berlin when the public jeered at the end of the first act of Verdi's *Don Carlo*, the conductor turned and announced in an icy voice, "The second act is no better than the first. So, if you didn't like the first, I'd advise you to go home now."

•

As the curtains parted for the last act of *Werther* in Palermo, the conductor, Giuseppe Baroni, looked for the tenor, but the prompter's box blocked his view. Stumped, he stopped the orchestra and began the third-act prelude all over again. With still no tenor to be seen, he crossed his arms and waited. At this, a gent in the fourth row said, "Why don't you go on, Maestro?"

Baroni replied, "The tenor is missing."

At that, several members of the audience pointed and explained to Baroni that the tenor was lying prone on the center stage. Baroni replied, "Oh, really? I didn't know anything about it." At this point another spectator chimed in, "Maestro, another little speech, please!"

•

Baritone Mattia Battistini loved to tell of a rival baritone's fate in *Un ballo in maschera*. After blowing his high note in the aria *Eri tu*, this stalwart rushed forward — before the audience had a chance to boo him, he shouted, "If you want to hear the rest of the opera, come over to my place." With that, he hightailed it out the stage door, costume and all.

•

About a century ago a nervous tenor was making his debut in Florence as Manrico in *Il Trovatore*. As the high-C in *Di quella pira* approached, his dry throat tightened and he knew he was about to scrog and that a scrog would nip his budding career before it could blossom. Thinking fast, he sang "...*madre, infelice, corro a salvarti. Aa...*" — and then, instead of the alpine high-C, he shouted, "*Vi-II-va Gariba-AAAL-di*" at the top of his lungs, knowing many would cheer and no right-thinking Italian would dare boo Italy's recent liberator.

•

From his first note in *Tosca*, tenor Galliano Masini's voice was scratchy. The audience whistled. At the end of the opera when the firing squad came out, Galliano yelled, "You guys should have come and shot me in the first act!"

•

On another occasion, Masini was singing beautifully in *Carmen* and his *Flower Song* received a tremendous ovation and shouts for an encore. He rushed to the footlights, motioned for silence, and said, "Please don't make me sing it again. It went so well the first time."

•

During a *Tosca* rehearsal for its premiere in Naples in 1914, conductor Leopoldo Mugnone became more and more impatient with tenor Emilio de Marchi. In the last act when de Marchi was in front of the firing squad, Mugnone yelled, "Soldiers, use real bullets."

•

At the end of World War II, allied troops in Vienna became adept at using PX goods, such as candy and nylons, to lure Austrian lasses away from their Austrian boyfriends. During *Don*

Giovanni, this state of affairs gave the Viennese bass baritone singing Leporello a chance to insert an ad lib that always evoked sympathetic chortles. After reeling off a long, impressive list of the Don's international amatory exploits — "in Italy 640, in Germany 231, 100 in France, in Turkey 91, but in Spain already 1,003 — Leporello would wink at the audience, and add in a stage whisper: "…and he did it all without chocolates or nylons."

•

In Parma in the 1960s a well-known restaurant owner and opera chorus member, Stigliano Barani, retired after a 30-year-long stage career. Stigliano was indeed a specialist. He sang only one small solo role: the Doctor in *Traviata*. For his farewell performance, the boys in the balcony decided to give Stigliano a send-off that he and the people of Parma would long remember.

The evening was remarkable indeed. Banners hung in the front of many boxes saying: "VIVA STIGLIANO." Whenever Stigliano came on or left the stage there were wild shouts of "BRAVO STIGLIANO" and stamping on the floor. Each time he dropped his jaw to sing, the whole opera was drowned out by hurrahs and stormy applause. As you might imagine, his entrance in the last act was greeted by a rip-roaring standing ovation from the top of the theater. Stigliano was fed up and fuming mad. So, when the Doctor's big moment came, instead of confiding to the dying heroine's maid that *"La tisi non le accorda che poche ore"* [The tuberculosis grants her only a few more hours], Stigliano rushed to the footlights and yelled, *"La signora sta benissimo."* [The lady is in perfect health] *"M'avete rotto i coglioni per trent'anni. Adesso vi saluto e me ne vado!"* [For 30 years you've pestered and pissed me off. Now I'm saying good-bye to you and clearing out of here!] Exit Dr. Grenvil.

•

Drinking their afternoon campari sodas, a bored group of young fops in Parma wondered if there were any sort of non-boring pastime they could find that evening. One suggested a typical entertainment for Parma "Let's go over to the opera and boo the tenor."

59

Several Parma opening nights on St. Stephen's Day have been totally wrecked by chain reactions ignited by various shouts from the balcony. In 1964 *A Masked Ball* turned into a "Masked Brawl," after audience insults aimed at the soprano had so irked the baritone that he yelled, "That's enough, you idiots," dashed off stage, refused to continue and was slugged by the general manager. The police were summoned and the opera folded in the middle of Act II. Then in 1979 a jinxed, sub-par *Traviata* evoked the yell, "You oafs!" and an invitation for the conductor to go into early retirement. Even the Mayor of Parma couldn't calm things down. So, when the noise of a loud, long fart rent the air during the Act II card scene, the theatre management decided enough was enough and the press officer announced that the performance was over.

Since the expectations of Parma audiences are much higher and greater than the availability of superior Verdi voices, this will hardly be the last debacle in Parma.

CHAPTER 7

TWADDLE IN THE FOYER

A Metropolitan box full of twaddlers in 1912

MORSELS OF IDIOCY HEARD out front make very popular small talk back stage:

"Come on, George, let's go."
"Why, honey?"
"Well, the program says the second act takes place several weeks later."
"Uh — will our tickets still be good?"

•

"We saw *Hänsel and Gertel* by Pumpernickel at the Blindborn Opera Festival."

•

After Walter Thuddington made his pile in oil and gas, nothing could keep Selma May Thuddington from buying the most expensive season box at the Oklahoma City Opera.

On opening night, after the first act of *Traviata*, she steered Walter toward the champagne-tippling luminaries in the lobby where she remarked for all to hear, "For such a young soprano she certainly has ungainly portamentos and a wide vibrato."

"Sugar," purred Walter, "ya took the words right outa mah mouth, an' that green dress made 'em look bigger'n all get-out!"

•

"We're going to hear *Tosca* next week. I can't remember who was the composer."

"Wasn't it Toscanini?"

•

"We're very sorry we can't come to dinner. You see, Thursday we're goin' to see *Tristan and Isolde*."

"Why don't cha jess bring 'em right along with ya!"

•

"Bel canto is gone"

"Where'd she go?"

"Where did *who* go?"

"Belle Canto."

•

At intermission in Tiflis, Georgia, one ticketholder [who thought he'd bought a ticket for Tchaikovsky's *Eugene Onegin*] asked his neighbor, "When does Lenski's arioso come?"

"It doesn't come at all."

"Why not?"

"This is *Carmen*."

"How stupid! I've wasted my money. I know every note of *Carmen*."

•

"We heard Chaliapin last night."

"Yes, we heard it last year. Wonderful cast."

•

"When we moved to Texas in 1965, if a singer didn't get a standing ovation, that singer had to be pretty bad."

— Gail White

•

"The only thing favorable we can say about future avant-garde operas is that none of us will still be around to hear them."

•

"This *Thaïs* is much too pornographic for me. Why, the singers are hardly out of bed long enough to sing anything."

•

"The second half of this program has something that sounds very naughty."
"Which piece are you talking about, Auntie?"
"That Sextette from *Lucia*."
"Auntie, don't you know what a 'sextette' is?"
"Of course I do, but I'd rather not talk about it."

•

"I'd like ta hear her sing Mimi's song by Pewk-ee-knee."

•

"How did you like last evening's performance?"
"I don't know. I haven't read the morning papers yet."

•

"Callas was simply stupendous in *Macbeth*, particularly in the Streetwalking Scene."

•

"For a *Carmen* with sex appeal who could really dance, I'll never forget old what's-her-name."

•

First Boston Dowager: "Why on earth did Tannhäuser abandon Venus?
Second Dowager: "You must have missed the point, dear. She wouldn't tell him her name."

•

At a reception for patrons and patronesses, an imposing lady remarked to a conductor, "I do love Puccini. Is he still composing?"
"No, Madam, I rather think he's *de*-composing."

•

"I don't know much about opera, but I know what I like."

"If you don't know much about opera, who CARES what you like?"

•

"That Radames tenor certainly doesn't look like an Egyptian General and his girlfriend Aida couldn't pass for an Ethiopian princess."

"Oh! How many Ancient Egyptian generals and Ethiopian princesses do you know?"

•

"I bought a recording today of Tosti's *Addio*."

"Is that from the opera *Tosti*?"

•

"Pinza's voice is so masculine. They say hairs grow on his vocal cords."

•

"I know you say you sing, but what do you do for a living?"

•

"Last year in Paris, we heard this same gal sing in *Faust*, but she was so awful they made her sing the jewelry song twice."

•

"How come *The Dance of the Hours* lasts only ten minutes?"

•

"No, George, it's called 'intermission,' not 'half time'."

•

"Boy, ya sure gotta hand it to her! She sang it like a regular Florence Nightingale."

•

I could not appreciate music in the twelve tone row because they gave me a seat in the 16th row.

•

"Last night this same company played Verdi."

"Oh. Who won?"

CHAPTER 8

DODO AND AENEAS
SUNG BY LILY PONSELLE AND EZIO PIZZA

"Do you have tickets for Puccini's *Tournedo*?"
"You must be joking, darling. *Tournedo* is by Rossini!"

Poor Dido, turned into a nincompoop! Poor Turandot, reduced to a hunk of steak!

•

PHONETIC CONSTRUCTIONS, such as *Lah-Beau-AIM*, *Air-NANNY*, and *Eye-EEE-dah* are supposed to help neophytes avoid embarrassing gaffes. Nonetheless, mangled names for operas, singers, arias, etc. are plentiful: *The Trail of Joan of Ark* by Norman Jello Doio and *Vietnamese Waltzes* by Strauss are mild examples. Ticket window people and record store clerks hear a great variety of such "misconscrewed" appellations. Just ask them.

How about Mozart masterpieces? *The Nozzle of Figaro*? The *Marriage of Fidelio*? *The Magic Carpet*? *Don Giovanna*? Or *Bastard and Bastardine*? This last was concocted by cast members who tired of rehearsing *Bastien et Bastienne*.

Another intentional misnomer for Donizetti's *Anna Bolena* was invented when a very heavyweight soprano took the title role — *Anna Balena* [Anna the Whale].

Then there was Stravinsky's *The Rape's Progress*. Nor should we neglect Mussorgsky's *Doris Godunov*, or Filippo Marchetti's *Ruy Blah*.

Some decades ago a New York FM radio station announced it was about to play the Overture to Rossini's *"The Seething Magpie"* [instead of *The Thieving Magpie*].

What about Willibald Gluck's *Orpheus and Uterus*?

Wagner, as usual, takes a tremendous beating. A bubbling-over Swiss fellow once stammered that his favorite Wagnerian works were *Lohenhäuser* and *Tannengrin*. *Tannhäuser* was justly nicknamed *Dann Heiser* [Then Hoarse] in honor of the many tenors and sopranos who forced their voices out of shape in that opera. A young Frenchman once turned *Les Valkyries* into *La Vâche qui Rit* [The Laughing Cow]. What about *Der Liegende Flohhändler* [The Reclining Flea Merchant]? Or *Der Ring der Niegelungenen* [The Ring of the Never-Successful]? The last link in The Ring has been referred to variously as *Goddammerung* or, by one critic, as *Goiterdammerung* — perhaps in reference to the way it was sung — or, as a German musicologist might have put it, "becowse Wagner vaz livink in Svitzerland ven he was compozing zuh Rring und zer vaz no iodized zalt in Svitzerland. Ferry bed for zuh Kropf … how you say in Enlish, uh, — zuh goiter."

Carl Maria von Weber's most famous opera was unquestionably *Der Schreifritz* [The Yell Fritz].

In Parma, a critic found the singers in Bellini's *I Puritani* so bad that he entitled his review *I Puri Cani* [The Pure Dogs].

The Puccini portfolio: In addition to *Tournedo*, he gave the world *La Bopeep*, *Johnny Squeaky*, *Manon Let's Go*, and *Madame Butterball* or, as Dr. Spooner would have put it, *Fladdem Mutter Bly*.

•

At a concert it was announced that "Nancy Tanner will now play 'The Meditation from Thee-ass'." My wife, the flutist, was so amused she could hardly pucker enough to play her instrument. A more common mispronunciation of *Thaïs* is "thighs." Whichever! Both Thee-ass and Thighs seem to fit the plot.

•

Aside from *La Tra-la-la-la-viata* or *La Triviata* and *Il Traviatore*, Verdi is responsible for that gut-buster *La Forza dell'intestino*, plus *Samson Boccanegra*, and *Her Nanny*.

Mascagni's most famous offspring has been renamed *Leon-cavallo Rusticana*, then rebaptized in a Viennese parody as *Krawalleria Musicana*.

In Milanese dialect, Georges Bizet is credited with *I Pesca-tori di Pirle*, which does not translate as *The Pearl Fishers* — but as *The Prick Fishers*.

Bedrich Smetana, as we all know, composed *The Battered Bride*, and Tchaikovsky's *Damned Pique*.

Then a Frenchman vilified Claude Debussy's *Pelléas et Mél-isande* as *Pédéraste et Médisante* [Pederast and Scandalmonger]. An English singer corrupted it into *Pelly's Ass and Melly's End*. In another French version, it becomes *Mélasse et Paliss-andre* [Molasses and Rosewood].

Last, but hardly least, a *New York Gazette* heralded the coming to town of Richard Strauss' ever-popular *Dr. Rosenkavalier.*

Now let's examine some deformed monickers such as Lily Ponselle and Ezio Pizza.

The 20th Anniversary of the Houston Grand Opera Company featured a gala concert, starring Beverly Sills singing with Sarah Caldwell conducting. At the splendid after-gala banquet, the president of the Houston Grand Opera rose and in high fettle saluted the honored guests."The Hew-ston Gray-und Op'ra Cumpenny has hay-ud a long-standin' love affair with Beverly Caldwell an' Sarah Sills."

In laughing reply, Beverly Sills said, "Worse has happened. Once in Chicago, a friend told me to go out front and look at the poster under the marquee. There diagonally across my ample bosom was a white strip of paper which read, 'Beverly Soils Sold Out'."

•

⌒⤳ Sometimes names are so out of all harmony with the owners' musical profession, you wonder why they didn't change them.

Howard Taubman — "Howard the Deaf Man" — A fabulous name for a music critic, don't you think?

•

Peter Schreier — "Peter the Yeller" — Hardly a great name for a tenor.

•

Contralto Lulu Mysz-Gmeiner (1876–1948) passed up the chance to change her name. So did soprano Deborah Strain. And what about the English contralto with the deep, deep voice, Dame Clara Butt (1873–1936)!

•

Do you suppose music by German composers Strungk (1640–1700) or Foertsch (1652–1708) was as mellifluous as their names?

•

It should be obvious why, after her Met debut, American contralto Eleanor Broadfoot (1878–1924) began to use the family name of her Cuban husband, Count Francisco de Cisneros. Tenor John Crow switched his to John Crain. No comment.

•

A contemporary German conductor with a budding international career changed his name from Christoph Prick to Christoph Perick before he came to America. Hmm!

•

Hungarian coloratura Maria Kempner had a novel idea: she took tidbits of her mother's name: [I]da [vo]n [Gün]ther and became Maria Ivogün (1891–1987).

•

German soprano Bertha Schwarz (1855–1947) not only transalpinized her name, she also bleached it: Schwarz [black] became Bianca Bianchi [White Whites].

•

Contralto Ernestine Rössler made her debut in 1876 in Beethoven's *Ninth Symphony*. By 1878 she was appearing in *Trovatore* in Dresden as Tini Rössler. Then she married the secretary of the Dresden Royal Opera, Paul Heink, and began singing as Ernestine Heink. That marriage was brief, but in 1894 she went to the altar again with a Hamburg theatre manager, Paul Schumann, thus allowing the opera, concert, and later the recording world to meet Madam Ernestine Schumann-Heink. Since her very ample figure was hardly "Tini," she also acquired the backstage nickname: Madam Human Shank.

•

To help fans pronounce his family name, Los Angeles tenor Archer Cholmondeley (1892–1966) changed the spelling to Chamlee — and added Mario in preference to Archer.

•

Emma Wixom (1859–1940) from Alpha, Nevada, had a name easy to confuse with "vixen." She launched her international career as Emma Nevada.

•

Perhaps the most bestial name change involved the great Spanish tenor Miguel Burro. Though with Burro his parents made an "ass" of him, he warded off quips about "braying" by changing his name to Miguel Fleta (1893–1938).

•

Spanish soprano Lucrezia Bori (1887–1960) of Met fame changed her name before her debut in Italy. Her original name had been Lucrecia Borjas. She was not only a namesake, but also a descendant of the infamous Lucrezia Borgia. Now, Borjas in Italy would be pronounced "borias," hardly a promising monicker for a soprano, since "boria" in Italian means "arrogance, conceit, ostentatious vanity."

•

Italian soprano Marisa Merlo may have felt she had to do something about her last name, which not only means "blackbird," but also in slang it stands for "simpleton, fool or dodo." She became Marisa Morel.

•

Danish baritone Lebrecht Hommel changed his voice to tenor and his name to Lauritz Melchior (1890–1973).

•

A fine dramatic tenor from Puerto Rico, Ermogene Imleghi Bascaran, may have been persuaded his name would look uncomfortable or insufficiently masculine on theatre marquees. At any rate, he changed it to Antonio Paoli (1870–1946).

•

Metropolitan opera tenor Charles Anthony has had a fine long career. His name at birth in New Orleans was Calogero Anthony Caruso. Any theories why he changed it?

•

Monicker modifiers in North America traditionally favor Italianate or WASPish names. Tenor Moses Adler of Polish birth became Norberto Ardelli. Jacob Pinkus Perelmuth became Jan Peerce (1904–87) and his brother-in-law, Ruben Tickner, became Richard Tucker (1913–75). Oklahoman tenor Joseph Horace Benton became Giuseppe Bentonelli (1898–1975), and tenor Alfredo Cocozza selected a more melodious and soothing combination — Mario Lanza (1921–59).

CHAPTER 9

OPERA IS SILLY AND I HATE IT

OPERA, FOR MOST OPERAPHOBES, is second-class music and third-class theatre. Let's listen to what they have to say:

"Of all noises, music is the least disagreeable" — nevertheless, "opera is an exotic and irrational entertainment."
— Dr. Samuel Johnson

Yes, my dear Dr. Johnson, we've heard you say that many times, but "no good operas can be sensible for people who do not sing when they are feeling sensible."
— W. H. Auden

"I look upon opera as a magic scene contrived to please the eyes and the ears at the expense of understanding."
— Lord Chesterfield

"Opera is a bizarre affair of poetry and music in which the poet and the musician, equally obstructed by each other, give themselves no end of trouble to produce a wretched result."
— Marquis de Saint-Evremonde

"We must remember that librettists the world over are apparently men of an inferior quality of intellect who know little about music or singing."
— Clara Louise Kellogg, soprano

"Anything in opera that is too stupid to be spoken is sung."
— Voltaire

"Nothing is capable of being set to music that is not nonsense."
— Joseph Addison

"Opera is strictly a matter of business. It's the selection of famous voices for fashionable ears. It has little bearing to art as art."
— Maurice Grau

"Whistle and do the shimmy, you'll have an audience."
— Diogenes, Greek Cynic (4th-Century B.C.)

"If an opera cannot be played by an organ-grinder, it is not going to achieve immortality."
— Sir Thomas Beecham

"The trouble with opera is that there's too much singing."
— Claude Debussy

"But nobody really sings in an opera; they just make loud noises."
— Amelita Galli-Curci

"Ah, how wonderful opera would be if there were no singers!"

— Gioacchino Rossini

"Where people sing, you can sit down safely — bad people have no song."

— An Old German Saying

"Swans sing before they die. Twere no bad thing
Should certain persons die before they sing."

— Samuel Taylor Coleridge

"The trouble with singers is that among friends and asked to sing they never will, but when they are not asked to sing, nothing can stop them."

— Horace, Roman poet (65-8 B.C.)

"Singers ought to be able to do anything, except bite off their own noses."

— Ludwig van Beethoven

Singers have "the wonderful ability for self-deception of all great performers, who believe anything they want to believe."

— Joseph Wechsberg

"Blessed are the arts which require no interpreters. The sun will never set on them."

— Arrigo Boïto

A singer is "a lover of myths and a convinced victim."

— Renato Capecchi, baritone

"What a blessing it would be if we could shut our ears as easily as we do our eyes."

— Georg Lichtenberg

"I have sat through an Italian opera till for sheer pain and inexplicable anguish, I have rushed out into the noisiest places of the crowded street to solace myself."

— Charles Lamb

Italian opera is "a special kind of art work, built on the brink of an abyss of ridicule, which is upheld by the force of genius."

— Bruno Barilli

"Italian audiences know exactly what they want in opera and, depending on what they get, lift you to the skies with their rapture or crush you to the ground with derision."

— Ezio Pinza

"Opera is like a mirror in which are reflected the dark sides, the large sentiments, the vitality and brigand side of the Italian character."

— Federico Fellini

"I have found opera tinged with such a mild but persistent form of insanity that nothing surprises me any more."

— Giuseppe Bentonelli, tenor

"One thing I don't understand: why in opera theatres do they let in spectators in the first three rows with musical instruments?"

— Alfred Jarry

CHAPTER 10

AREN'T YOU JOAN SUTHERLAND?
NO, I'M BEVERLY SILLS

AS TOLD IN HER MEMOIRS, soprano Leontyne Price was asked by a passerby, "Aren't you Joan Sutherland?"

"No," beamed Leontyne, "I'm Beverly Sills."

•

Since opera performers earn their living pretending to be someone else, is it any surprise that they relish mistaken identity, incognito, and impostor yarns?

Basso Luigi Lablache (1794–1854) was hardly a midget. In his stocking feet he was a six-foot-four, 330-pound giant. The apartment he rented happened to be one floor below his exact physical opposite: the famous American circus midget, Tom Thumb.

One Saturday, while his servants were out, Lablache answered a knock at the door and found a startled Englishman. The Brit surveyed Lablache from head to toe and stammered, "the ...the midget, Tom Thumb?"

Drawing himself up to his full magnificence, Lablache smiled and with a courtly bow and a flourish of the arm worthy of W.C. Fields, he announced, "I, sir, am Tom Thumb."

"But on stage ...I mean, you were so ...small, and you ...uh ...had the voice of a cricket," gabbled the stranger. "Ah, yes!" Lablache purred, "On stage, kind sir, I *have* to be that way, but when I'm at home — I can LET ...MYSELF ...OUT!"

•

One afternoon, baritone Adolfo Mariani, the former owner of Asti's Restaurant, that Lower Manhattan eatery where singers congregate and sing, was reminiscing about singers of yesterday. He had a particularly vivid story about Titta Ruffo, "the Caruso of the baritones." During a lunch with Ruffo at Viareggio near Ruffo's hometown of Pisa, he and Ruffo were making animated comparisons of baritones past and present when their elderly waiter interrupted, "You *signori* know NOTHING about baritones. You haven't even mentioned the greatest of them all, Titta Ruffo, who comes from my hometown, Pisa."

"Oh, come off it!" blurted Ruffo, "Compared with Riccardo Stracciari, Ruffo's voice was a fart!"

The waiter grew pale then crimson with rage, and he bolted into the kitchen. Ruffo and Mariani, gasping with laughter, then decided it was cruel not to let the old fellow in on their fun. They had the headwaiter coax him out of the kitchen. Mariani introduced a laughing, apologetic Ruffo. Tears of delight came to the old fellow's face, and he kissed his idol's hands — both of them.

•

On his first concert tour in the United States, pianist Jan Paderewski was honored in Austin, Texas, at a joint session of the state legislature. Paderewski made a few polite remarks and was heartily applauded. Then, as the clapping subsided, a white-haired legislator rose from his seat and begged the pianist, "Please, suh, we beseech y'all to favor our assemblage with a song."

CHAPTER 11

IS THERE A THROAT DOCTOR IN THE HOUSE?

SORE THROATS! OPERA FOLK KNOW that next to the ego, the most troublesome spots in a singer are the larynx and vocal cords areas. Bad throats — real, imagined or faked — are the most common excuse for a last-minute cancellation. A prima donna may both have and be a pain in the neck, but the pains she causes management and her colleagues are much lower.

General manager Giulio Gatti-Casazza came from La Scala to the Metropolitan Opera in 1908 after many colorful years dealing with manic opera artists. He was to have many more.

Around the 1920s, tenor Giacomo Lauri-Volpi phoned to croak that he had an awful throat and couldn't sing that evening. "So what else is new!" Gatti mused to himself, but purring sympathetically, he told the tenor to get some rest and not to worry about a thing. A little later, he phoned back and told Lauri-Volpi that Beniamino Gigli — Lauri-Volpi's archrival — had graciously agreed to take the part that evening. After wishing him a speedy recovery, Gatti hung up.

Within half an hour Lauri-Volpi was back on the line. "I'm feeling much better and my doctor says I can sing tonight myself." Gatti had not even bothered to phone Gigli.

A savvy opera manager knows his wards, knows most often the singers with the healthiest bank accounts are the ones who call in sick. Several questions zoom through an opera manager's mind when a singer calls in. Is the bad throat perhaps just acute jitters, or a ferocious hangover, or a bruised ego? Is there some little vendetta going on? Has the artist recently been acting quirky? Or, unlikely as it may seem, does the singer have an honest-to-God sore throat?

•

Whenever singers get together, small talk eventually turns to pills, gargles, injections, inhalations, and the favorite throat guru in this or that opera town. Star throat mavens are highly paid and in great demand. And, like their fickle clientele, a couple of brand-new medical stars rise each year while some old stars sink below the horizon.

Throat specialists' anterooms are often plastered with photos with flowery dedications and touching allusions to rescued careers. If these are recent photos of top-of-the-line singers, then physician's fees are usually top-of-the-line as well. But such high stipends are often well earned. A throat man's work for opera singers is by no means limited to killing germs and soothing inflamation. He must also be a father confessor, psychologist, mentor and pal. Transoceanic calls at odd hours are par for the course: "Doctor, I cannota seeng. You musta 'elpa me. Dee peels, dey do notta work." So, throat specialists sometimes take expensive emergency trips to wherever the singer may be to administer injections, inhalations, or whatever else he or the patient believes in.

•

Singing as if she had just gargled with steel phonograph needles, a Bulgarian soprano announced to the audience, "I yam a leetle horse, becows I heff a leetle colt."

•

Speaking of injections, one New York throat man and long-time favorite of singers was jabbing a needle into the bare bottom of Russian soprano Luba Tcheresky when her husband casually remarked, "You must have seen a lot of famous derrieres in your day, Doc."

"Yes, I have," mused the specialist, "and it sure beats peering down inflamed throats!"

•

Back stage in Torino, frantic yells from the tenor drew cast members out of their dressing rooms. "Help! Get me a doctor! I've been poisoned." The tenor was careening down the corridor, holding his pants up in front, but with his bare bottom showing behind.

His wife, it turned out, had accidentally injected into his buttock, a vial of medicine for the aerosol machine instead of the look-a-like vial of vitamins.

•

A star soprano suggested to a young German medical student who loved opera, "Why don't you become a throat specialist? That way you'll always have free opera tickets." To his chagrin, once this student's fame for respiratory cures was established, his first patient was a rock star and his only offer of a free ticket was to a rock concert.

•

Tuscan tenor Galliano Masini had gone through rehearsals for *Aida* in Rome, but early the morning of the first performance he woke up with a throat that felt really awful. He tried singing a few notes, but his voice came out completely scratchy. Very worried, he phoned his local Roman throat man, Dr. Motta. The doctor dashed over and looked down his throat, and said, "I'm going to spray your throat with some medicine. Stay here in your room, take it easy, keep quiet, take a rest, don't speak or sing a note, you'll see that when you get on stage tonight, your voice will be in great shape." Masini did as he was told and to his delight he was in superb voice from the beginning to the end of the opera.

After the final curtain, Dr. Motta came back to his dressing room. Elated, Masini thanked and complimented him most profusely. Motta replied, "By the way, there was nothing wrong with your throat this morning. It was all in your mind. That spray I used was merely distilled water."

•

Italian tenor Edoardo Garbin really believed in pills. This creator of tenor roles in *Falstaff* and *Zaza*, this man who sang Rodolfo in the first successful production of *La Boheme* had a special pill for each register: one for high notes, another for low notes, and a third to help his middle register. He even had special pills for loud and soft singing. Late in life, as a voice teacher in Milan, Garbin passed on his pill philosophy to his students. Among them was Polish tenor Jan Kiepura, who kept his registers registering using the same pills as his Maestro.

•

This brings us to a common throat ailment known as "the pianissimi of Chaliapin." Since many singers racket about to all hours of the night, carousing, shouting, singing, and carrying on, some discover the next morning they can coax only croaks from their cords. By mid-afternoon they may be able to push out a few loud notes, but soft tones and diminuendos? Forget it! If the evening's role demands lots of trailing off into pianissimo, they can try gargles, pastilles, and the like, but if these don't work, why not resort to a Chaliapin *pianissimo*?

Chaliapin was a consummate actor. He could spellbind listeners even if, after a night on the town, his cords were swollen and debauched. By keeping his mouth open, knitting his brows, and slowly raising his hand as if to guide some upward wafting sound, he convinced his listeners they were hearing ethereal tones. His stage colleagues, however, knew no sound whatsoever was coming from the basso's throat. Critics too sometimes raved about "the *pianissimi* of Chaliapin."

•

The saddest throat tale of all involved the most celebrated voice of the century: that of Enrico Caruso. [This story comes from Mario del Monaco.] When Del Monaco reached the Met in 1950, there were plenty of old-timers around New York from Caruso's era. Del Monaco milked them for all they knew about his admired predecessor. Several of them told him that Caruso's early death at age 49 probably was hastened by a medical blunder by Caruso's friend, Dr. Mario Marafioti, the Met's house physician.

Late in his career, Caruso's throat, like the gullet of many other singers, was more and more easily irritated, which meant more days of rest between performances. To protect his throat, Dr. Marafioti prescribed anti-inflamatory medicines suspended in mineral oil. Del Monaco learned that Caruso took to spraying his throat with an atomizer whenever he came off stage. After several years of inhaling mineral oil mist, puddles formed in Caruso's lungs. Doctors were not yet aware that mineral oil is an irritant that the human body does not absorb. Pleurisy and abcesses followed. Caruso had lung surgery twice, but died at the age of 49 in 1921 still in his artistic prime. If this story is accurate, the most celebrated singer of the century may have been done in by his own doctor. Actually, the debate about what malady led to his final lethal surgery in Naples has never really been settled.

CHAPTER 12

ALCOHOL, TOOTHPICKS AND OTHER PROFESSIONAL HAZARDS

ALCOHOLISM IS HARDLY A RARE THEATRE DISEASE. So, let's look at liquor before going on to more exotic hazards, such as peppercorns, onstage bladder and bowel emergencies, and even murder.

Carlo Cartica was a nice, laid-back fellow with a tenor voice of rare beauty. He was superb whether in heavy or light tenor roles and his high notes bloomed gloriously. He had just one little drawback: he was always drunk. Reality, to Carlo, was merely an illusion created by a lack of alcohol.

For a *Lohengrin* in Santiago, Chile, he turned up in the wings even more soused than usual. As he lurched and nearly fell stepping off the Swan Boat, the stage director swore, crossed himself, and bit his nails. The prompter cued Cartica with the word "*Mercé*" for Lohengrin's first line. Now, since "*mercé*" is a high-flown Italian way of saying "thank you," Cartica grinned, turned to the prompter with a courtly bow and said, "*Mercé anche a voi.*" [Thanks to you, too.] The prompter froze and playful Cartica, not recalling what he was supposed to do next, began swatting the swan's head back and forth.

Down came the curtain. Stagehands wrestled Cartica to the wings for a tongue lashing and a potful of espresso. Then Cartica was catapulted back on stage and the opera resumed. Threats of being fired and blackballed had sobered him up fast and for the rest of the evening he sang and behaved like a true Knight of the Grail.

Eventually, Cartica's love affair with liquor forced employers to invent ways to keep him dry or at least sober enough to walk in a straight line, but they were no match for the thirsty singer. Finally, his skunk-drunk antics had riled so many managers and agencies that no theatre wanted him, beautiful voice or no.

Then, one theatre manager had a brainstorm — a sure-fire way to use Cartica, yet keep booze and the singer away from each other. The contract specified that, except when escorted on or off the stage, Cartica would eat, sleep, and live locked in an upstairs theatre dressing room suite from the day of the dress rehearsal until the last curtain of the final performance. Since weak finances were interfering with his guzzling, Cartica sighed and signed. His agile mind had already figured out a way to get whatever hooch he hankered for.

The plan was simple. A fan brought a gift basket of gourmet goodies to his dressing room, with a coil of rope hidden in the folds of a tablecloth. Cartica thus could lower the basket out his window into an alley, where, by prearrangement, a lad from a local wine shop would load it with any potables Cartica required. The third performance was already over before Cartica was caught in a hoist and the riddle of his perpetual tipsification was solved.

•

Sweden's wonderful tenor Jussi Bjoerling was also a devotee of strong waters, a taste shared by his colleague and friend, conductor Nils Grevilius.

One day, after a colossal binge in Oslo, the pair boarded the train to Stockholm, loaded almost to the point of amnesia. In the dining car they downed a few more scotch and sodas and debated what to do when the train reached Stockholm. Grevilius pointed out, "It's your town, Jussi. You decide."

"Well, we've eaten already and they roll up the sidewalks in Stockholm after dark, so I guess the only thing we can do is drop by the Opera and see what's cooking." And so they did, settling into rear row seats just as the lights went down. Then something very strange occurred: instead of the conductor, out to the footlights came the general manager, who announced the performance would have to be cancelled, because "the conductor Nils Grevilius and the tenor Jussi Bjoerling are missing."

Astonished and glassy-eyed, Grevilius and Bjoerling struggled to their feet, waved and shouted in chorus, "No! No! Wait! We're right here! We're here!"

Very few in the stolid Scandinavian audience smiled.

Towards the end of his career, they say some theatres added a clause to Bjoerling's contracts: if he failed to show or was too pie-eyed to perform, he had to pay a hefty fine. He died at age 49 of heart trouble, probably abetted by alcohol. [The Bjoerling family does not recall this incident, but granted the indulgent habits of Bjoerling and Grevilius, this event could well have happened. Even Bjoerling's most fervent admirers in Scandinavia joked about his love of scotch.]

A third tenor much bedevilled by booze was also a Swede: Arnold Lindfors, better known as Aroldo Lindi. He too died young, perhaps thanks to years of over-imbibing.

Often drunk as a hoot owl, he could sing magnificently even though he had to hang on to furniture to keep from falling on his face. Making his debut in Italy as a last-minute substitute, he lurched out of the wings for Don Alvaro's dramatic first act entrance in *La Forza del destino* and astonished everyone, and particularly the soprano, by rushing over and hugging not her, but her maid, Curra.

•

In Florence opera buffs recall a local baritone who downed a bottle of wine before each act to "steady his nerves." Sometimes he dozed off in his dressing room and/or on stage.

In *Rigoletto* during the second act, after this baritone's vengeance aria, he plunked down on a chair, with elbows on the table, and heaved massive sobs while Gilda sang her aria *Tutte le feste al tempio*.

Sobs soon changed to massive snores. Everyone could see that old Rigoletto was out like a light. The orchestra went *um-pa-pa, um-pa-pa*, but our wino-baritone snored peacefully on. Gilda gave him an elbow in the ribs. That merely jarred his snoring. She pinched and shook him. He just turned his head, smiled, and dozed on. By now the public was snickering freely. Finally, Gilda banged her fist as hard as she could on the table right next to his ear. That explosive bang got his attention. He bolted upright, very befuddled, and belted out Scarpia's first line from *Tosca*, "*Un tal baccano in chiesa!*" [What an uproar in church!]

•

Igor Stravinsky did not become an alcoholic, but he loved scotch whiskey so much he said his name ought to be changed to "Stravisky."

•

Ancient Roman poet Horace indirectly praised composers who drank when he wrote, "Songs composed by drinkers of water will not please nor survive for long."

So much for alcohol. Let's look at some other equally dangerous pieces of opera equipment: rapiers, swords, spears, daggers, and even conductors' batons.

London's *The Spirit of the Times* of April 11th, 1840 contained the following item:

"A tragic event occurred a short time ago at the opera theatre of Lucca, during a performance of *Lucia di Lammermoor*. A rivalry had been for some time existing between two of the performers, and a duel had taken place, but they apparently had been reconciled. In the second act of the opera, however, during the combat, their former animosity revived as they thrust at each other, and the stage fight became a real duel. The public in the meantime applauded their earnestness without suspecting its cause. Suddenly, the artist performing the part of Ravenswood uttered a dreadful cry, for he had received a wound in the chest, and then fell dead upon the stage. The other singer was immediately arrested. The company, unwilling to appear again after this melancholy event, broke up on the following day, and the theatre remained closed."

•

On the less tragic side, a stage director in Germany found an ingenious way for the spear in *Parsifal* to arrive in the tenor's hand. The spear would simply come up at the right side of Parsifal through a hole in the stage. The only trouble was one night the tenor did not stand in the right place and the spear came up not in his right hand, but into his crotch.

•

Mad King Ludwig II of Bavaria (1845-86) had a favorite Lohengrin, namely Cavaliere Arturo Scovelli. Scovelli, incidentally, was an American, Arthur Scovell, born and bred in Detroit. Since Ludwig could spend the royal purse almost any way he pleased, he built a meter-deep pond in the theatre of Linderhof Castle so he and a few pals could admire Scovelli standing in full armor on a Swan Boat belting out Lohengrin's final aria. During one encore of this aquatic favorite, Scovelli lost his balance and pitched into the drink, heavy armor and all. He would surely have drowned had not His Majesty and some musicians hopped in quickly and yanked Lohengrin up for air.

•

Thumping out rhythm on the floor with a long staff or cane was about all the early orchestra conductors were expected to do. The baton had not yet been invented. Such a staff proved the undoing of the "French" composer and conductor Jean-Baptiste Lully, who was actually a Florentine baptized Giovanni Battista Lulli (1632-87).

One day in a fit of rehearsal pique, Lully pounded his staff down hard and wounded his right foot. An abscess and blood poisoning finished him off.

Incidentally, at Lully's deathbed a father confessor told him he would have to burn the manuscript of his recent opera, unless he himself wanted to burn in hell. Lully promised he would and, indeed, he had the manuscript burned, but not until he had had it copied and placed in the King of France's library. As the Italian saying goes, "As soon as the law is invented, a way around it is found."

•

During a towering rehearsal fury in Torino, Arturo Toscanini broke a violinist's bow. A sharp end flew into the violinist's eye and blinded him. He sued Toscanini for a healthy sum — and won.

•

Mental illness can be a danger in any profession, but paranoic schizophrenic soprano Lina Bruna-Rasa as Tosca struck real terror into her Scarpia when she lunged wild-eyed at him with a stiletto. For safety's sake, the baritone grabbed her hand and guided the knife to his own chest, thus becoming the first Scarpia to commit suicide.

•

Even without swords, knives and daggers, some opera roles seem very unhealthy. The fiendish title role in Cherubini's *Medea* (1797) earns high marks as a health hazard. The first soprano to sing the role, Julie Scio, is said to have wrecked her lungs singing it and died. A few years later, *Medea* drove Clara Stökl-Heinefetter out of her mind, and demented she remained for the rest of her days.

•

In 1889 Maestro Franco Faccio prepared and conducted the first performance of *Die Meistersinger* in Italy. The strain of intense rehearsals drove him berserk. He was put in an asylum, where he died a year later.

•

French mezzo Simone Berriaux's opera career was curtailed in an unusual way. Toscanini considered her the best voice of the century for the role of Mélisande. One night on the Riviera at an after-opera dinner, she was eating steak *au poivre* when a peppercorn got stuck next to her vocal cords. She coughed bloody murder. It wouldn't come up. In the morning a surgeon removed it, but the darned pepper had burned her cords so badly she was never able to sing well again. A career ruined by a pepper seed!

•

Can a toothpick ruin an opera career? It might if you do what La Scala basso Marco Stefanoni did. According to his nephew, Uncle Marco chose to pick earwax out with a toothpick, but distractedly left the pick in his ear. When he went to bed and rolled over, he drove the damned thing through his eardrum. When the punctured drum healed, he could no longer hear the orchestra properly and had to retire from the stage.

•

The famous suicide jump off the battlements of Castel Sant'-Angelo at the end of *Tosca* has often led to a variety of jokes and accidents. Several decades ago at the Met, a soprano had pestered the general manager for years to let her have a shot at Tosca. Finally, Johnson — or was it Bing? — gave in and this lady threw herself over the parapet with such elan that she broke two front teeth. When the reigning queen of the Met Toscas, Zinka Milanov, heard of the incident, her only comment was, "How many time I tell dat vooman not to try dee dramatic parts!"

A young soprano asked a great diva, "How do you sing Elektra?"

"You make sure to go to the toilet before going on stage," was the terse answer.

•

Yes, throughout opera history urgent intestinal and bladder problems in mid-scene have been rare-but-dreaded hazards. Long roles such as Elektra are an open invitation to inopportune accidents. In such long operas, orchestra players are at an even greater risk. In fact, the first thing orchestra members inspect in a strange theatre is not the acoustics, but the shortest route to the WC.

Incidentally, during most of the four centuries opera has been around, toilets in theatres simply did not exist. Singers brought their own potties. Adelina Potti — excuse me! Adelina Patti — made do with two potties: one in her dressing room and another backstage behind the scenery. For the public's convenience [?], ushers carried buckets around and collected a tip for their use. While the show was going on, in the corridors servants of the wealthy didn't even bother to use buckets. Strongly perfumed handkerchiefs and bottles of scent came in handy to help listeners disregard pungent aromas. We seldom realize how lucky we are to be living in the era of the flush toilet.

Even in the middle of the the last century, assaults on olfactory nerves were distracting in some theatres. Many noses will remember the reeks in German theatres right after the Second World War. In Munich's unheated Prinz Regenten Theatre during winter 1947-48 it was so cold you could see your breath. Nevertheless, nothing could keep Bavarian opera lovers away. They filled the place wearing their wool or fur overcoats over many layers of clothing. The pervasive odors were a combination of potatoes and onions fried in pork fat, boiled cabbage, very bad tobacco, schnapps and beer, plus a sickly smell of stale sweat. Aroma wasn't built in a day. What price music! But we're wandering off the subject of toilet emergencies on stage.

•

Roly-poly little soprano Lina Pagliughi had a minor flaw that mischievous colleagues loved to exploit: she laughed easily, and when she laughed, her bladder valve often malfunctioned. Unchivalrous cast members competed to see who could make her leave puddles on stage.

In *Lucia* one night, a killingly funny aside made her lose both bladder and rectal control. As luck would have it, Edgardo that evening was that irrepressible Tuscan Galliano Masini, who sensed keenly what had happened.

The next time they sang *Lucia* together, he changed Edgardo's entrance greeting by one letter: instead of singing "*Lucia, perdona*" [Lucia, pardon me], he sang "Lucia, merdona." [Lucia, you big shitter.]

•

When Lynne Strow Piccolo sang *Norma* at Covent Garden, she noticed after a long-drawn-out scene that one of the youngsters who huddled around her as Norma's children had quietly piddled a puddle.

•

Piano accompanists say the act of straining for high notes or bowing to the public has driven some singers to unintentional flourishes of flatulence, of which two of the pianist's four senses become keenly aware.

90

Moldy, choking dust clouds waft up from many an old stage, especially during changes of scenery. What a treat for singers with allergies! Though theatres have installed modern misting mechanisms to wet down the dust, in most older provincial theatres with short seasons performers face the hazard of coughing and wheezing in mid-aria.

A German baritone had no sooner come to rehearse in musty Po Valley theatre in Cremona when his allergies blossomed into a storm of sneezes. He asked the management to please, please get rid of the dust. He was assured the problem would be taken care of immediately as soon as the rehearsal was over. The next morning the dust was as bad if not worse, so, between coughs, he repeated his request and got the same *"Si, signore. subito!"* [Yes, sir, immediately!] The dust, however, was just as thick the third day, so he bought and ceremoniously donated to the theatre management a vacuum cleaner.

Opera can be a very damp profession when you are playing opposite a singer who spews spittle in moments of intense passion. Tenors Francesco Tamagno and Pasquale Brignoli were prize spewers.

As Tamagno at La Scala was leaning over ostensibly dead Romilda Pantaleoni in the last scene of *Otello* and yelling, *"Desdemona! Desdemona! Ah, morta, morta,"* she said under her breath, "Listen, kill me, but stop spitting all over me or I'll get an umbrella."

•

Brignoli was an even more notorious expectorator. Singing Don Ottavio in *Don Giovanni,* he was warbling and spitting away at the side of Donna Anna and Elvira. Donna Anna this particular evening was Francesca Lablache, a last-minute substitute. Since she had no costume for the part, she wore an expensive Worth gown made in Paris, which Brignoli was generously spraying with mouth mist. Finally, Francesca whispered to him in French, "Let's see, *mon cher ami*, if you couldn't manage once perhaps to spit a bit on the dress of Elvira."

•

Large, heavyset and hammy as an actor, the great tenor Francesco Tamagno loved to make very theatrical lunges to dramatize his ear-shattering high notes. He would clench both fists, raise them just in front of him to elbow height and then when he attacked the high note, thrust both fists forward and take a lunging step toward the footlights, stamping his left foot hard on the stage. All well and good, until in an ancient Po Valley theatre he stamped and his leg went right through the stage up to the knee. Stuck there, the curtains closed and carpenters had to hack and pull him out.

CHAPTER 13

DUMB AS A TENOR — VAIN AS A PRIMA DONNA

"Let's sing the duel ...oops! I mean the duet."

LEAD SOPRANOS AND TENORS usually appear on stage as lovers, whereas in real life it's often just the opposite. Who is the star of this show anyhow? And who has the better voice? You or I?

Francesco Marconi (1853–1916) had been a carpenter before becoming a star tenor. When he arrived late for a rehearsal of *Les Huguenots*, soprano Fanny Torsella sneered at him. "Well, Signor Marconi, you *are* a carpenter, aren't you?"
"Yes, madam, I am, and I should be delighted to make your coffin for you — GRATIS."
•

Many sopranos agree the best act for the tenor in *Madam Butterfly* is Act Two. The tenor is not in that act.
•

93

Back in the 1920s, Columbia University decided to build the Casa Italiana, a center for Italian studies and culture, quite fitting for the only metropolis that had almost more people of Italian blood than Rome itself. Adolfo Mariani, a baritone best known as the proprietor of Asti's Restaurant in Lower Manhattan, was chosen to shake the operatic money tree. The first singer he approached was the highest paid Italian at the Met, tenor Beniamino Gigli. After a little arm-twisting, Gigli agreed to give $100.00. Adolfo then dashed over to the apartment of Gigli's arch rival, Giacomo Lauri-Volpi, and said Gigli had contributed $200.00. "I'll give $400.00," Lauri-Volpi blurted without a second's hesitation. Back careered Adolfo to Gigli, "Lauri-Volpi is giving $800.00." "What!" yelled Gigli, "I'll give $1,000.00."

This back-and-forth continued until Mariani had badgered roughly $1,500.00 from each tenor — all of which bears out the old Italian saw: "Between two litigants, a third party is the winner."

•

General manager: "We need you tonight. Your colleague who was to sing Florestan tonight has the flu. He cannot sing.

Tenor: "What you say about the flu is news to me."

Tenors' jokes most frequently have to do with dunderheadedness or conceit. Backstage, few would contest the truth in the old saying: "men, women, and tenors." This is perhaps why Jean de Reszke, the Met's leading tenor in the 1890s, often said, "I am not a tenor. I'm an ex-baritone."

An old theory claims tenors' brains shrivel after several years of high notes. But do not knock tenors because they lack gray matter: they need that empty space for resonance.

•

According to Leo Slezak, himself a tenor, a young fellow's brain was damaged. So he sent it out for repair, but then forgot about it. No matter: a voice coach discovered his tenor voice, so he didn't need a brain.

•

At the end of *La Boheme* after Mimi dies, the tenor is supposed to cry out in anguish, "Mimi! Mimi!" but this tenor didn't
sing those words. Asked why, he said, "I know it's hard to believe, but I couldn't remember her name."

After the third performance of *Otello*, at a banquet the Otello
tenor was seated next to his soprano Desdemona. Halfway
through the main course he turned and said, "You know, I rather
like this opera, but there's one thing I don't understand. It's so
silly. Why does Otello get so damned excited about a mere handkerchief?"

Conductor: "We'll do *Di quella pira* half a tone down so
you won't have to worry about the high-C's."
Tenor: "Not to worry, Maestro. No matter what the orchestra
does, I'll sing the high-C."

Speaking of high-C's, during a performance of the *Barber
of Seville* dark-voiced baritone Titta Ruffo, on a bet, put in an
interpolated high-C. He held it for what one listener swore was
almost half a minute. Result: his voice was out of whack for
days, but he had proved that he had a loftier range than some
tenors.

•

Jan Kiepura from Poland had a splendid voice and some
exemplary tenor foibles. Only a few days off the boat from
Europe he had his first New York encounter with the press.
One questioner asked, "Mr. Kiepura, they say you are an egotist.
Is that true?" Kiepura replied, "Egotist?!? Not the great Kiepura!"

In California, Kiepura once confided to fellow tenor Vin-
cenzo Cimmarrusti, "Compared with me, Caruso was nothing."

The wife of a Polish conductor, Artur Rodzinski, recalled
that when young Kiepura was at the beginning of his career in
Poland singing minor roles, he once lurched forward holding

on endlessly to a clarion high note as he walked across the stage to the footlights. This feat brought down the house and launched him into important roles and a stellar career.

•

Tenor Lauri-Volpi had just sung a fine concert in Stockholm and was leaving the theatre with his accompanist, Luigi Campolieti. At the stage door, a fan yelled, "Oh God, how I wish I could sing like you!" Standing on the top step and staring down, Lauri-Volpi replied, "Well, try! By all means, try!"

•

On returning to Germany, a tenor told his wife, "I wanted to buy you a calendar with stupendous photos of the California coast, but didn't."

"Why not?" she asked.

"We couldn't use that calendar here. California time is nine hours later than Germany."

•

During *Tosca* at the Met, Richard Tucker whispered to Maria Callas,

"Relax, Mary, you're in the big time now."

•

Singers often try to glean hints from other artists about a particular role, scene or aria. The hints they get are not always enlightening.

Richard Tucker was rather new at the Met when Edward Johnson urged him to study *Andrea Chenier*. Shortly thereafter Tucker was seated at a banquet right across from Giovanni Martinelli, who had been a famous Andrea Chenier. So, Tucker ventured, "Giovanni, tell me about some of the little ins and outs of *Andrea Chenier*. Johnson asked me to learn the part." Martinelli stared at him for a moment and simply said, "Easa very gooda fora dee voice." That was all.

In reality, *Andrea Chenier* has been anything but good for some tenor voices. In 1920 this opera was in preparation at the Met as a vehicle for Caruso, but he was too ill to take it on. So,

Beniamino Gigli sang the title role, but after a couple of performances, Giovanni Martinelli had to sub for him. When Caruso learned Gigli had cancelled, he commented, "Yes, Gigli came down with a bad case of Andrea Chenitis."

Mario del Monaco held a press conference just after he came to the Met in 1950. This was a year when there were four or five other famous Italian tenors singing in New York. A newswoman asked him, "Whom do you consider your greatest rivals in singing today?"

"The question is absurd. I've only two rivals: Caruso and Gigli and they're both long gone from the stage." [Asked the same question in Italy, he added the name of Tamagno.]

In New York a journalist was interviewing a French tenor:

"What do you think of Mario del Monaco?"

"Italian peeg!"

"What about Jussi Bjoerling?"

"Swedish peeg."

"What about Lauritz Melchior?"

"Danish peeg."

"What about Leonard Warren?"

"Such a bee-you-tee-fool bahreeton voice."

If anyone told Richard Tucker a particular singer was very good, he was known to say, "If they're so good, how come they haven't sung with me?"

When asked about her rival, one soprano gave this appraisal: "If she had in her upper register what she's lacking in the lower register, she'd have a good middle."

Singer's Agent: "You have an extremely high falsetto range for a tenor. Are you by any chance a castrato?"

Singer: "That's a 'privates' matter."

Fan: "You're the greatest and most perfect soprano singing opera today."

Soprano: "No, that's not true. No, certainly I am not perfect — but I'm the only good one."

•

At the Tri-City Opera in Binghamton, New York, Myron Fink's opera *Jeremiah* was well into rehearsal when a female principal singer came up to the composer and inquired, "Tell me, how does the opera end? What happens?"

Taken aback, Fink exclaimed, "Haven't you read the score? It's all in there. Just read it."

"Yes, yes! But I'm not in that part of the opera."

•

A fan asked Zinka Milanov what opera would be on at the Met next Thursday. She answered, "How could I possibly know? I'm not singing on Thursday."

•

A diva's comment about her rival, "Her problem is not the 46 inches around her middle, but the six inches between her ears."

•

Soprano: "Rivals give me fits."

Mezzo-soprano: "But you're so in love with yourself, how could you possibly have any rivals?"

•

One soprano to another: "I really can't understand why the audiences' applause was so feeble and the stagehands were grumbling. I thought you sang your very best."

•

First Diva: "I want to do *Aida*, and I want to do it in the worst way."

Second Diva: "I'm sure you will."

•

First Soprano: "You can't imagine how much singing a heavy Wagner role takes out of me physically, mentally and emotionally."

Second Soprano: "If it's so hard on you, why do you bother to do it?"

•

"The critic was very insulting. He compared the way I sang Dalilah with a fire engine. He wrote that I sang it 'like a true siren'."

•

A soprano boasted to her rival, "I've been asked to sing at three funerals next week."

"Well," came the reply, "at last you've found people dying to hear you."

•

Asked why so many other sopranos said bad things about her, the prima donna replied, "If I've enemies, it's their fault and not mine."

•

The soprano interrupted, "Let's not talk about me. Let's talk about YOU. What do YOU think of ME? — But before that, why don't we listen to the tape of my Los Angeles *Rigoletto*?"

•

A soprano was asked for her frank opinion of the mezzo-sopranos in the company. She replied with a riddle, "How many mezzo-sopranos does it take to change a light bulb? None. They can't. It's too high for them."

•

How many divas does it take to screw in a light bulb? Just one.

She holds the bulb and the world revolves around her.

According to critic Manuela Hoelterhoff, "this is a true diva....Convinced of her specialness and totally uninterested in what any one around her was doing."

•

When a prima donna thinks about other singers, she recognizes three kinds of egotists: first of all, the kind that fancies she can sing as well as SHE does; second, any others who boast about their own voices and careers and give the prima donna no chance to talk at length about HER voice and HER career; and third, anyone who is not thinking of her at that moment. *Avid* is just *Diva* spelt backwards.

•

Sopranos and castrati throughout history have given the world blazing examples of conceit and petulance. Though castrati couldn't make children, they sure could make trouble, and, like the castrati of yore, many a latter-day soprano has found it useful to act like a brewing tornado or a bomb waiting to explode. Some have felt ill-hidden joy when they create incidents and confusion. Probably no one on the boards today could match Maria Callas for crisis-fomenting bravura. When someone commented on her knack for churning up hectic situations, Callas replied, with an ennui worthy of Greta Garbo, "Everywhere I go there is chaos."

•

An elite, top-drawer Italian opera troupe crossed the Atlantic in 1931 bound for the Colon in Buenos Aires. Baritone Titta Ruffo was the most famous singer in the group and Galliano Masini was the star tenor. The singers were gathered one evening in the ship's first-class lounge for coffee, liqueurs and conversation. Out of the clear blue sky Masini spoke up, "Tell us, Commendatore Ruffo, after Caruso, who is the world's greatest tenor?" Maybe Galliano thought Ruffo would name him, but Ruffo replied, "One fart from Caruso would drown out all the tenors active today."

Chapter 14

Applause Hogs, Scene Snatchers And Saboteurs

Have you ever wondered during curtain calls, why singers hold hands? Holding hands simply prevents any applause-giddy singer from lurching forward for a solo bow. Ah, solo bows and applause-hogging! The problems and jealousies they have created!

•

American baritone Lawrence Tibbett made his Metropolitan debut on January 2nd, 1924 as Ford in Verdi's *Falstaff*. At the end of the performance, the audience gave him a hefty round of applause. At this point, however, Antonio Scotti, in the title role, did a very stupid thing: he came out for a solo bow, thinking the applause was for him. The audience reacted with "shouts, whistles and catcalls" and an interminable ovation and yells for Tibbett. The opera simply could not continue until Tibbett had his solo bow.

Scotti did not make the same blunder in the second performance — and there was no ovation for Tibbett.

•

Nellie Melba late in her career made a similar gaffe. An Australian audience was clapping during her final bow and shouting the young Italian tenor's name: "Martinelli, Martinelli, Martinelli!" Nellie graciously came out alone to accept this applause, and the yelling increased. Later she explained she had thought her fans were yelling, "Auntie Nellie, Auntie Nellie!"

•

For an all-star Montreal *Otello* in the 1960s, Mario Del Monaco was Otello, Renata Tebaldi, Desdemona, and Aldo Protti, Iago. At the second-act curtain, there were several cries of "BRAVA" for Tebaldi. When the bows were over, Del Monaco froze and then flew into a towering rage, shouting at Tebaldi, "You idiot! You've paid the claque!" Del Monaco then stormed straight to his dressing room, locked himself in, took off his

101

costume and makeup. His wife begged him to go back on for the last act. Nothing doing. Then the theatre manager tried to get him at least to open the door — no go. After various other ploys, somebody remembered that a young Canadian was in the theatre and had a knack for bringing Del Monaco out of deep blue funks. So, the young fellow was summoned, briefed and implored to save the situation.

He knocked on the dressing room door and said, "Maestro, it's I. Can I come in?" To everyone's surprise, Del Monaco opened the door and without a word let him in. "What a great disappointment for the audience, which came from far and wide and paid for a chance to hear the great Del Monaco." Del Monaco shook his head. The young tenor tried another four-square appeal to Del Monaco's vanity. It also fizzled. Nothing worked. Suddenly, the young fellow noticed a large book on Enrico Caruso resting on the dressing table. He had often heard Del Monaco speak very admiringly of Caruso both as a singer and as a man. So, he pointed to Caruso's photo on the jacket and said, "What would HE think, Commendatore?"

Del Monaco leaned back to mull the question over and suddenly said, "All right. Tell them I'll come out in a little bit and finish the opera."

•

Mutual distrust among opera folk has always been strong, since a few have tried to enhance their own careers by undercutting their rivals via fibs, exaggerations, and innuendoes. George Bernard Shaw noted that "No one in the profession dreamed of believing fully in the public statements of their colleagues."

Riling rivals in the wings just before their cues to go on stage is a tried and true maneuver, the ideal opportunity for bitchcraft and sabotage.

An Italian tenor was warming up his resonances backstage — humming, mouthing words, and feeling his nose bone and skull for vibrations. Suddenly, a stage assistant handed him a telegram that read, "YOUR WIFE DIED AT TEN THIS MORNING." Concentrating hard on his warm-up, he simply used the telegram words as an exercise mantra, saying over and over again, "TUA MOGLIE È MORTA ...uh ... M . O. .RTA ... MORTA." So, the sabotage fizzled because — being a tenor — the meaning of the words never penetrated.

•

"I heard you Monday night. What was wrong? Were you sick?"

•

Rival: "Do you feel you'll be able to hack it tonight?"
Bass: "I'm ready and in good shape. No sweat."
Rival: "Well, that's good, because you aren't very good, you know."

•

When baritone Tito Gobbi made his debut in Cairo in 1949 as Rigoletto, he knew he'd be singing for a public that idolized his Florentine rival Gino Bechi. A few minutes before curtain time, a telegram arrived at the theatre saying, "THE GREAT ITALIAN BARITONE GINO BECHI HAS DIED STOP. THE ENTIRE NATION IN MOURNING." The cable, read aloud to the audience, sure took the bloom off Gobbi's debut. A second telegram arrived two hours later saying that Bechi was in Trieste alive and well. Other cast members heard Gobbi mutter over and over again, "These damned Tuscans!"

•

During rehearsals for the world premiere of *Otello*, Verdi commented to his lead tenor, Francesco Tamagno, about the French baritone singing Iago, "Maurel makes a very good Iago, don't you think?"

"Yes, Maestro," Tamagno replied, "Even on stage."

•

Emma Calvé as Carmen was having an offstage feud with the tenor, so when he dropped his jaw to begin Don Jose's *Flower Song*, she stuffed a whole rose into his mouth, thorns and all. In another production, Carmen sabotaged her Don Jose by rubbing and crushing the rose all over his fat cheeks while he tried to sing.

•

In still another *Carmen,* at the end of the love duet, Carmen was seated while Don Jose rested his head in her lap. During the applause, the tenor raised his head and nodded his thanks and smiled at the audience. At that, Carmen grabbed his bullneck and jerked his cranium back into her lap. Still squeezing his windpipe, she whispered, "Do that again, you fat bastard, and I'll throttle ya."

•

Singers love telling stories about how they got even with any colleague who upstaged or sabotaged them. Baritone Giuseppe de Luca liked to recall that after Lily Pons had tried to snatch a scene from him at the old Met, he bided his time and had his revenge in a later act when he was supposed to hug her. He suddenly squeezed her ribcage hard and turned her high note into a barnyard squawk.

•

The possibilities for onstage pranks and sabotage are almost infinite. Put itching or sneezing powder in your enemy's wig or fake beard. Mix a little ground glass in the cold cream. Hide a key prop. Write rib-cracking or scurrilous obscenities on a scroll or in a letter your colleague must open and read aloud.

In *Don Pasquale* the heroine Norina opened her book only to find a condom in it. When Lady Macbeth opens a letter she has been known to read assorted vulgarities, but she tries to sing the words in the libretto and not laugh.

•

Bice Adami Corradetti recalled a *Girl of the Golden West* in South America where a fat baritone in the part of Sheriff Rance sat down on a cane-bottomed chair that split, leaving him with his hip bones wedged tightly below the seat and unable, even with help, to rise from the chair.

•

In the last act of *La Boheme,* a prankster stuck a warm Modena sausage in Mimi's fur muff and all on stage watched soprano Rosetta Pampanini try to keep a straight face as she sang, "Oh, how beautiful and soft it is. Is it you who give it to me?"

•

As the dying Mimi, self-important diva Nellie Melba was tenderly placed on the bed in the last act of *La Boheme,* but as the bedcovers were lifted to cover her, the audience burst into hysterical laughter. Under the bed there was a large potty. Caruso had the stagehands put it there.

Melba often chewed a wad of Australian evergreen gum to keep her throat moist. Just before going on stage, she would plunk the gum into a cup in the wings. Then when she came off, she would plop it back in her mouth. One evening while she was on, Caruso had the gum replaced with a wad of chewing tobacco. As she came off, Nellie tossed it into her mouth, grimaced, gagged and spat.

•

Fyodor Chaliapin had the unendearing habit of telling everyone from conductors to stagehands what to do and where to get off. So, in Monte Carlo in 1916 in *Don Quixote* after this huge bass was helped up onto his mule, a stagehand jabbed a hatpin into the mule's rump and Chaliapin became a rough rider on a would-be bucking bronco. He did not, however, give his saboteur the satisfaction of falling off.

•

A 1984 Bayreuth the *Ring Cycle* the stage direction of Sir Peter Hall included in Act III a long, transparent water trough about a meter deep to allow shapely Rhein Maidens, stark naked, to swim across the stage. This attention-grabbing novelty proved even more grabbing at dress rehearsal.

Just before curtain time a male chorister was seen dipping his hands in the Rhein Daughters' aquarium. No one gave this a thought. Then all of a sudden, all three nude swimmers began shrieking and the rehearsal came to a screeching halt. The dipper had dumped six frisky bullfrogs in the tank to keep the girls company.

•

In Mainz in 1993, *Griechische Passion* by Czech composer Bohuslav Martinu (1890-1959) was on the docket. This unusual work had roles not only for singers, but also for a goat and a donkey. A docile donkey was easy to find, but a docile goat? An ad in the local paper lured several goat owners with their nannies and billies for an audition. A sweet, calm little female named *Zwiebel* [Onion] won the audition, partly because the score stipulated, rather preposterously, that the goat have horns and yet give milk. Zwiebel was producing milk and attaching a couple of horns would be no problem.

At her first rehearsal Zwiebel was escorted to the makeup room half an hour before the curtain to have her horns mounted. On stage she behaved very well and even seemed to like being there, but when a cast member sang the line, "Do you like to eat onions?" as if on cue she bleated "beh-heh-heh."

Now, her big scene required she be milked by the soprano during that soprano's aria. But how to keep her standing still for just the right length of time? Her owner suggested feeding her favorite food, barley, but she wolfed that down too soon and headed offstage to see where she might find more. So, choosing the right amount of the right fodder remained a dilemma. Her owner suggested trying eight dried bread rolls, but that didn't work either because her loud munching and crunching drowned out the soprano. Fresh rolls were the eventual solution.

Zwiebel and the donkey stole the show and were quite popular with the press as well. In fact, a reviewer wrote a long article about the two bestial scene snatchers with scant commentary about the opera itself, the composer, or the singers. Several days later the same paper published a mock interview with Zwiebel and her asinine co-star.

A Versatile Opera Prompter

CHAPTER 15

OPERA SEX — MASCULINE, FEMININE AND NEUTERED

HATS OFF TO GERMAN SCIENTISTS who find things to measure no one thought of measuring before. In the 1980s researchers Eberhard Nieschlag and Wolfgang Meuser finished a study on 102 male singers and confirmed scientifically what many a woman and cuckolded husband knew already: the deeper a man's voice, the higher his level of sex hormones — and sexual encounters. They also confirmed that lower-voiced males generally have athletic builds, whereas tenors tend to be fatter, shorter, and rounder. [So what else is new?] Moreover, tenors, they found, have a lower level of offstage sexual activity, even though paradoxically, on stage they're the guys who get the girl. So, Mozart again was smarter than most: his world-class libertine, Don Giovanni, was a bass-baritone, whereas he wrote a light tenor part for the wimpish Don Ottavio.

By the way, this research project was no joke. It was written up in a German medical journal, *Sexualmedizin.*

Couldn't these fine men of science delve further into two more hormone-measuring projects? First, the study of the many spinto and dramatic tenors who started out as baritones. Did they uphold their reputations as ladykillers even after they became tenors?

Another measuring project comes to mind. Do deep contraltos have more estrogen than squeaky little soubrettes?

•

Going back to *Don Giovanni* for a moment, Arturo Toscanini approached baritone Paolo Silveri around 1949 and said with enthusiasm, "Silveri, we must do *Don Giovanni.* I'm sick and tired of always the same Don Giovanni. Pinza! Pinza! Pinza! That's a part for a baritone, not for a bass. The baritones are the real lovers, the real Don Giovannis. The basses are good only for doges of Venice or Genoa and cuckold husbands."

Many singers firmly believe male voices lose sheen and vigor if their owner has had sex too near performance time. But *what* is too near? One week? One hour? True-life stories on this *leitmotif* are often gleefully told by prima donnas. As a matter of fact, prima donnas have been known to sabotage their primo uomo partners by luring them into bed or into their best friend's bed the night before, or better yet, the day of the big performance.

Here's another thing to measure: what percentage of university music departments, conservatories, and voice coaches teach this sabotage tactic to future prima donnas or warn their male students about the pitfalls of romancing too close to curtain time?

•

Asked if she refrained from sex before singing, Birgit Nilsson said, "I refrain from sex? No, I'm not a tenor."

•

"A good sex life is the best thing for a woman's voice."
Soprano Leontyne Price.

•

Journalist: "What about sex before a performance?"
Tenor: "Too risky. Made me late once for my entrance cue."

•

In 1944, baritone Titta Ruffo claimed he laid off sex once for as long as six weeks before a crucial performance, "for the sake of my art." His tone of voice and eyes raised to heaven showed what superhuman sacrifices his art demanded.

•

Here is a bit of anatomical doggerel to underline the main point Eberhard Nieschlag and Wolfgang Meuser were making:
A light tenor has no balls,
A lyric tenor has one,
A lirico spinto has two,
A Heldentenor also has two, but he's stepping on one.

•

When Met tenor Jean de Reszke (1850-1925) retired and taught singing in Paris, a tenor pupil asked his advice about sexual abstinence before a performance.

"Men ought to stop for maybe two or three days before-hand."

"What about women?" the student asked.

"Well, at least they shouldn't do it on stage," de Reszke replied.

•

A poverty-striken father of a wealthy castrato begged his son for money. The son said, "All right, dad, I'll repay you in kind" — and handed him an empty purse.

•

Luigi Ricci (1805-59) was prolific not just as a composer of comic operas. He was also famous thanks to the beautiful Bohemian twin sopranos who became his mistresses. He claimed they looked so alike he could not tell them apart. This was probably true: he had four children by one and five by the other. There is more than one theory why Luigi went insane and died so young.

•

Neapolitan opera composer Leonardo Vinci (1690-1730) had a vast following in Rome, including a very beautiful Roman noblewoman, with whom he began a passionate affair. Through the grapevine the noble lady heard that Leonardo was bragging all over town about their bedroom frolics.

She had her revenge by a hot beverage spiked with arsenic. Thus ended Vinci's brilliant career at age 41.

•

A tenor came home too early and found his baritone pal in bed with his wife.

"What are you doing?" he screamed.

"Well, in September I'm doing *La Boheme* in San Francisco and then in November *Rigoletto* in Chicago," replied his pal, casually lighting a cigarette.

•

Asked why he gave up studying for the priesthood, tenor Giuseppe di Stefano answered simply, "I like de girls.".

Finding, wooing, and winning a mate is a key theme in human life as well as in opera. If you believe that opera plots mirror human behavior, then you have to admit that courtship habits in northern climes are slow, shy, and ever so slightly clumsy, compared with, say, Italian, French, and Spanish wooing routines. An Italian bass, Aldo Reggioli, summed it up:

"In the time it takes a Wagnerian tenor to kiss his beloved, any Verdi tenor would have had her pregnant."

A multi-talented Italian baritone Afro Poli developed a naughty artistry as a Peeping Tom and was much esteemed by male colleagues. When he drilled peep holes through hotel room doors or walls, he magnanimously allowed his cronies to peep along with him at some shapely young female disrobing or a couple making love. These voyeur escapades alleviated boredom while lolling in hotels between rehearsals or performances.

In Toulouse, in the 1960s, an Italian company was giving a series of operas at the Capitole Theatre. At the hotel our inventive baritone had spotted a handsome, lovey-dovey pair, seemingly on their honeymoon. He saw which key they picked up at the desk and while they were out sightseeing, he unlocked their door with his skeleton keys and found their bed was just a few feet from the door. So, with a confederate down the hall to warn of approaching traffic, he drilled two holes, swept the sawdust up, filled the holes with removable wooden plugs, and camouflaged his handiwork with varnish.

That evening when the young people went to their room, he and five cronies tiptoed down the hall and took turns at the peep holes, but as they pressed ever harder against the door, it suddenly flew open and all six pitched forward, landing in a big pile half on top of the unfortunate couple. Trying to unscramble and get the hell out of there, the tenor lost his hairpiece. Although the toupee was expensive, he did not ask the hotel management to retrieve it.

Some castrati were also famous ladykillers. Eighteenth-century ladies of fashion found them attractive bedroom buddies because they were great celebrities and social lions, and, most important of all, there was no danger of pregnancy.

The fleshly singer playing Julius Caesar was not only shaped like a capon, he was cut out as a boy to *be* a capon. He was the famous castrato, Francesco [Senesino] Bernardi. The opera was Händel's *Giulio Cesare*. The year was 1724. The place — The Royal Academy of Music in London.

Senesino had just blasted out the phrase, "Caesar knows no fear," when a backdrop fell behind him with a hideous crash. Senesino hit the deck in terror. There, to the audience's delight, lay fearless Caesar, moaning, shaking, and quaking like a frightened child.

•

The gender of the singer taking this or that role in the days of the castrati was moot and required much "willing suspension of disbelief." Sure, modern audiences can swallow Cherubino sung by a mezzo-soprano, imitating a young man who is masquerading as a girl, but could today's public put up with a three-in-one situation where a eunuch sings the part of Hercules and then suddenly sheds his outer garment to reveal that he is really a woman pretending to be a man?

•

The Pope in Rome whose edict banished women from theatre stages to preserve public morality was actually a colorful, reactionary Milanese whose standard way of turning down any new idea was to utter or write one word in his dialect, "*MINGA*" — meaning "absolutely not." By modern standards, this pope was certainly a male chauvinist pig. He even decreed that women should dress very chastely to restrict their sex appeal. He believed that a woman on stage had about as much chance of retaining her virtue as she would have of falling into the Tiber and not getting wet.

Italians nicknamed this Pope "Papa Minga." Ironically, his papal name was Innocent XI. Ironic, because his edict led to the castration of many thousands of Italian boy sopranos in order to replace female singers on stage. It was dangerous for a boy with a fine soprano or tenor voice to be born into a poorer family, for it was frequently easy to convince his parents that once castrated he might become a famous singer and bring the family untold wealth. In one year alone, over 4,000 Italian boy sopranos and altos were castrated in hopes they would achieve fame and fortune. Very few did.

•

Giovanni, a factory worker in Empoli just south of Florence, came home and found a stranger in bed with his wife. In utter rage, he killed her and spent the next four years in jail for this "crime of passion."

In jail he learned barbering and opened a barbershop in a nearby town when he got out in 1932. Things went well for him until one day, lathering a gent for a shave, he recognized his wife's lover and began furiously singing the famous line from *Norma* "At last you are in my hands." [*In mia man alfin tu sei*], stropping his razor in time with the music. The client got the picture instantly and bolted down the street closely pursued by the shrieking barber, brandishing his razor.

In   mia man _____ alfin tu se __ i

CHAPTER 16

THE RIGHT PHYSIQUE FOR THE ROLE?

IN THE AGE OF HOLLYWOOD AND TELEVISION, casting tiny tenors as great leaders of men and very matronly ladies as winsome teenagers is only a bit rarer than before. Over the centuries, singers who looked too portly or too puny have provided what you might call a motherlode of humor.

The world premiere of *Traviata* in Venice in 1853 was a famous fiasco, partly because fat Fanny Salvini-Donatelli was miscast as Violetta, supposedly dying of an emaciating disease. The public jeered her and the tenor and baritone as well.

In another *Traviata* in sedate old London, tubby, squat Luisa Tetrazzini caused a critic to comment that "she looked as if she had dropsy instead of TB." Tetrazzini's favorite response to such comments was, "Some gotta da figure. I gotta da voice."

•

Six-foot-four, 330-pound basso Luigi Lablache (1794-1854) was once cast as a prisoner wasting away in a dungeon. The first words he sang brought down the house: "I'm starving."

Is fat necessary? Must you be pear-shaped to emit pear-shaped tones? Have abundant fat and abundant hormones something to do with opulence of voice, as some authorities claim?

As mezzo Marilyn Horne explained to students at a University of Texas master class, "you don't have to be super-fat to be a super-star, but an awful lot are."

•

Fred Gaisburg, recording engineer for His Master's Voice, began his long career just before 1900 and recorded most celebrity voices in the first half of the last century. Noting early on that most big voices come out of big bodies, he came up with an explanation: "Mass gives tone. As with an instrument, so with the voice. You cannot possibly have a grand piano without a grand frame to show it off."

•

Stout Hilda Konetzni was singing Venus in *Tannhäuser* in Vienna. Her overblown form draped on a couch prompted one American spectator to ask another, "When do ya think the balloon'll go up?"

•

When Maria Callas first auditioned for the Met, she was offered the role of Madama Butterfly by Edward Johnson, but she turned it down because she felt she was far too fat for the part. She weighed nearly 200 pounds at the time.

•

Comedian Jimmy Durante, who was also an opera buff, claimed he particularly liked the part in the second act — he never said which opera — "when de 300-pound soprano sez to de 100-pound tenor, 'hug me, honey, hug me.' Why, ta hug 'er, de bum would have ta be coyved like a banana!"

•

After the first rehearsal, the small tenor complained that the soprano's forearm was bigger than his thigh. When this same soprano wearing chain mail suddenly turned on him in rapture, her armored breastworks hit him square on the chops and knocked him flat on his miniature rump.

•

Richard Strauss really threw casting directors a curve ball: how do you find a German soprano with the right physique for *Die Frau ohne Schatten* — The Wife without a Shadow?

•

Baritone Titta Ruffo had the upper body of a bull, but the mirror told him his legs looked awfully scrawny in tights. Calf muscle padding sewn into his tights took care of the problem. He had a good laugh after a performance of *Hamlet*. Two young ladies barged into his dressing room looking for autographs. Spotting his padded tights hanging on a hook, one said with great disappointment, "Look over there. Those are the baritone's legs."

As Shakespeare might have said, "Nothing is big or fat but eating makes it so," and few opera singers are known for self-denial at the dining table. A singer's last meal before the show is usually taken several hours before curtain time because thorough digestion gives more space for inhaling deeply and cuts down the chance of burping or toilet anxieties in mid-aria. Since the physical and nervous exertion of a big role burns lots of calories, singers usually stoke up before and after.

Adolfo Mariani of Asti's restaurant in New York, said that when king-size tenor Lauritz Melchior stopped in for an after-hour snack, he ordered and polished off first a platter of sliced ham and salami, then a big bowl of pasta, followed by a mountain of meats and a big salad. To top it off, he ate some rum cake — not a slice, but the whole damn thing.

Adolfo then asked, "Mr. Melchior, would you like some coffee?"

"Yes, Adolfo. Espresso. Espresso."

"With sugar?"

"No, Adolfo. Saccharine! Saccharine! Do you vant to poison me?"

CHAPTER 17

WHY NOT GIVE A RECITAL?

*"Last night we heard a hippopotamus
that had swallowed a canary."*

RELATIONS BETWEEN SINGER AND ACCOMPANIST can be quite
good or rather touchy. They need each other, but each sometimes damns the other with very faint praise. Singers have been
heard to complain that in an accompanist "you either can have
notes or you can have sensitivity, but you can't have both."

Accompanists, for their part, say some singers aren't even
musicians. Anyone can sing, but to play the piano you have to
practice, study and be able to read music. They mightily resent
instinctive singers, such as Ezio Pinza, Fyodor Chaliapin, tenor
Galliano Masini and many others who rose to the pinnacle of
international fame and fortune with negligible skill at reading
music. How could that happen?

Yes, just like Pinza, Livorno tenor Masini reached La Scala, the Met and other important theatres, but when a conductor asked him why he could not sight read, Masini sneered that no one should expect him to be able to decipher "those little specks of fly shit."

·

In Edinburgh, piano accompanist Gerald Moore had just sat down at the piano to begin his first important concert outside England. He was nervous. Just as he was about to put his hands on the keys, the soloist, the Canadian soprano Pauline Donalda, upped his tension further by leaning over and whispering, "Not too loud."

Then, as he began to play the intro of her first song, she leaned over again and murmured under her breath, "But not too soft."

·

Singer to accompanist: "Could you transpose the accompaniment *down* a full tone from A-flat to B-flat?"

·

Prima Donna: "I'm so nervous. I want to be alone and not see anybody."

Her Rival: "Then, why don't you give a recital?"

·

In the 1920s an American soprano married a minor French Count with a major bank account. Being public spirited, she offered to give a concert for charity in his hometown. So, with noble husband in tow, she examined the auditorium, and tested the acoustics and the piano.

"François," she announced, "the piano is much too high. It's disgraceful. Unless they lower it, I simply refuse to sing. I'm going back to the château for a nap, please stay here, and insist they do something about it."

Around five the Count arrived home quite tired. "They didn't want to lower it, but I insisted and paid for it, and it's done."

When soprano and accompanist arrived at the hall they found roughly two inches had been sawed off each leg of the piano. [The Count apparently had never heard about pitch.]

•

Another energetic American soprano in Europe early in the last century was Lucy Hayes of Newark, New Jersey — Lulu to her friends. She was a niece of President Rutherford Hayes. She had married an Italian tenor, Angelo Minghetti, and spent the First World War with him in Rome. Like the American soprano in France, she too was public-spirited. To do her bit for the war effort she tried to put together a benefit concert for the Italian Red Cross. She and her tenor husband approached their friend, Neapolitan baritone Enrico Pignataro, to join them.

"Enrico," said Hayes, "you must help. In the first half of the program I'll sing an aria, you'll sing an aria and my husband will sing an aria. Then we'll do a duet or two and a trio. We'll be doing a simple act of philanthropy."

"Signora Lulu, you know for you I would do anything, but I must say no. An act of *Philanthropy*? I do not know this opera *Philanthropy*, or even who wrote it."

•

Ezio Pinza suddenly needed a piano accompanist for a recital in San Francisco because the one he was counting on had taken ill.

On the telephone with pianist Gelen Lurwick, the sub, they talked over the program and Pinza bemoaned that he was missing the music for *Di Priva*.

Gelen was mystified. Was this possibly a song by Tosti or someone of his ilk? He phoned Sherman Clay and several other music stores, but no one had ever heard of *Di Priva* as a song or a composer's name. A bit sheepishly he called Pinza back and said, "I'm terribly sorry Mr. Pinza, but I cannot find this music in all San Francisco. Who is the composer?"

Pinza replied, "Bot eet ees an American song. Everybawdy knows eet, 'Dee-ee-ee-p Reever', my home ees over Jordan."

•

Then there is the perhaps apocryphal yarn about a soprano in recital who was making one mistake after another. Each time she goofed, she would glare at her poor accompanist. He just sat there stoically and played, but as they were leaving the stage he "accidentally" stepped on the train of her gown. Her skirt ripped off, leaving her careening for the wings in her undies.

•

A New York socialite warned her accompanist at the rehearsal before her little recital, "There'll be no encores. I don't believe in encores. However, — if the audience insists, you must drag me back on stage. Do you understand?"

During the program, there was polite applause, but after her last song, her brother and an accomplice began yelping, "ENCORE! ENCORE!" Immediately, she said to her pianist, "All right. Drag me! Drag me!"

•

After dinner in Milano, the hostess' Sicilian brother insisted on singing *O tu Palermo* from Verdi's *Vespri Siciliani*. His voice, as bad luck would have it, was wobbly and wandered off pitch in all directions. Nevertheless, half way through, tears started rolling down an elderly dinner guest's cheeks and her shoulders heaved with sobs. His artistry had obviously touched her deeply. He rushed over and asked, "Are you Sicilian too?" "No," she moaned, "I'm a musician."

•

Basso Chaliapin was a night owl and a carouser if there ever were one. So, when Henry Ford's family tried to lure him with a fat fee to come to their Dearborn, Michigan, home to sing a couple of arias at a 10:30 a.m. Sunday brunch, Chaliapin cabled back, "Unfortunately, at that early hour I cannot even spit."

•

The addled program chairman of the Thursday Morning Music Club rose and nervously announced, "Miss Gwendolyn Jones will now sing "God knows why" and Mr. Playbody will pee for her."

•

A matinee idol baritone in Boston agreed to come with his accompanist and give a program of six arias and one piano piece at a society matron's hoity-toity brunch. The fee: $2,000.00, but when she added, "You're not expected to mingle with my guests," he replied, "In that case, our fee will only be $1,500.00.

•

A tenor named Hotchkiss was about to sing for the Tuesday Morning Music Club. Possibilities for botching his name were many. Madam President made one of her usual, coy introductions. "And now, ladies, I have a simply marvelous surprise for you — a very special treat. A young tenor with a fabulous career ahead of him will sing for us. — Now, the second part of his name reminds us of love. I wonder if any of you can guess it. — No? Well, then, it is my great pleasure to introduce Mr. Hitchcock."

•

The newsletter of a Hemet, California, retirement home announced that, "Mrs. Gwendolyn Buckley will sing a program which includes the popular selection from *Madam Butterfly — Un bel dick.*"

CHAPTER 18

I TEACH *BEL CANTO*
THE OTHERS TEACH *CAN BELTO*

"Palate up ...larynx down!"

HOW DO YOU SING TO PRODUCE *bel canto,* and what is *bel canto* anyhow? Much fur has flown trying to answer those questions. The most famous 19th-century voice teacher of *bel canto* was long-lived Manuel Garcia II (1805–1906), who not only pioneered the scientific study of voice, but also wrote several important treatises and invented the little round laryngoscope mirror so beloved by dentists. Many of his students and their disciples became superstar singers and teachers. They in turn watered down Manuel's lore and passed it on to their pupils.

Garcia tried to describe simply and straightforwardly how singers ought to breathe and produce the first note in a phrase.

Ever since, voice teachers have disagreed vehemently about what he meant. As singers have long noted, teachers disagree about a lot of things. Some teach students to open their mouths wide. Others say that's dead wrong. Breathe through your nose. No, breathe through your mouth. No, inhale via both nose and mouth. When you breathe, imagine inhaling through a flap in the back of your neck. Breathe through your forehead. Sing through your eyes. It's pretty confusing. Push down with your shoulders as you inhale. No, pull up your shoulders around your ears as you inhale and push down slowly as you sing. No, no, relax your shoulders and do nothing with them. Hold your chin way up and tilt your head back when you sing. No, tuck your chin down. No, keep chin and head level. Tilt your head over toward your right shoulder when you sing. The Maestro who gave this last bit of advice had a node on his vocal cords and found tilting his head helped him. Many of his students without nodes aped him and always tilted their heads to the right when they sang.

Playwright George Bernard Shaw's mother was a singing teacher. Shaw recalled that voice teachers of her era never agreed on much of anything. A typical teacher would refer to all others as "impostors, quacks, voice smashers, ignoramuses, rascals and liars."

•

Ex-singers who take up voice teaching often scorn any voice coach who never sang professionally. The same is true in reverse. A famous teacher in Milan, Maestro Arturo Merlini, was a non-singer but he had accompanied and coached famous singers since he was a teenager. His conservatory degree was in piano and his opinion of ex-singers as teachers went like this: "When a singer develops vocal problems in his own voice and cannot correct them, he now feels qualified to teach others."

•

For the past 75 years voice teachers have been at pains to explain "how Caruso did it": how he used his diaphram, jaw, tongue, larynx, uvula, lips, butt muscles, etc., etc. Only one thing is clear ... had Caruso used all the techniques attributed to him, he would have gagged on the first note.

•

Teacher: "What music did you bring?"
Student: "I brought four arias."
Teacher: "Well, which composer shall we have turn over in his grave today?"

•

Early in the last century, a certain Italian Maestro Ciccarelli found a surefire way to boost his students' enthusiasm. He had his older daughters rap on the studio door in the middle of a lesson. The maestro would ask them brusquely why they were interrupting and the oldest would exclaim wide-eyed, "But, papa, we didn't know you had Caruso studying with you!"

•

Neapolitan conductor Leopoldo Mugnone (1858–1941) retired to Florence in 1920 and gave singing lessons. His hearing had failed so badly that he had to stop conducting. Frank Chapman, the husband of Met mezzo Gladys Swarthout, began studying with him. Mugnone tried to teach him the baritone role in *Traviata*. One day after a session, Mugnone rose from the piano bench and, standing solemnly in front of a large portrait of Verdi, said ever so softly, "Papa Verdi, forgive me for giving lessons to this baritone, but I have to eat, you know."

•

Silas Mills did the stylish thing for a man of good, solid Massachusetts stock: he sailed off to Europe around the turn of the century to study with Giovanni Lamperti (1839–1910), renowned teacher of such international superstars as David Bispham, Ernestine Schumann-Heink and Marcella Sembrich. After the Maestro had assessed his voice, Mills inquired what the Maestro thought about his career possibilities. Lamperti replied calmly, "Well, you can sing in church."

After two years of lessons with Lamperti, Silas repeated his question and the answer was, "Well, you can sing in church."

When Silas returned to America, he ended up conducting church and university choirs — at Smith College, for instance — and he sang solos in church.

·

Perplexed, the voice student asked why his teacher always sidled over to the open window wherever he, the pupil, sang. "I'll do it so no one down in the square will think *I'm* the one that's singing."

·

Maestro Merlini in Milano was wont to say, "I never accept homely or ugly women as students. I tell them they sing off pitch and there's nothing I can do for them."

·

Asked who was a good singing teacher, Met general manager Giulio Gatti-Casazza replied, "A good singing teacher is simply one lucky enough to find a pupil with an exceptionally beautiful natural voice — and not ruin it."

·

Some teachers would rather slit their students' throats than have them switch to some other teacher. Singers therefore take great precautions to keep their teacher from finding out they are taking lessons elsewhere on the sly. An Italian baritone in mid-career asked tenor Luigi Ottolini to relay to Maestro Merlini his desire for Merlini's help in solving some upper-register problems. He added, "But tell Maestro Merlini no one must know that I am taking lessons from him." When Merlini heard of the proposition, he told Ottolini, "Tell Signor X that I agree with him completely: I would never want anyone to think he had studied with me."

·

Caruso liked to tell of a teacher who brandished an umbrella as a teaching prop. Opening the umbrella was the signal for the student to sing EEEEEEEE-AAA, and when he closed it, AAAA-AAAA-EEE. Perhaps he was the same fellow who said, "dee voice–eh mossa be jossa likea dee ombrello: opena, botta covered."

Here are a few more props voice teachers have used: wine corks — you sing while holding one between your front teeth; small corks — plug your nostrils with them so you'll have to breathe only through your mouth; wooden tongue depressors — to keep your tongue down, grooved, sideways, or to prop your teeth apart; pencils — great for tweaking the uvula with so it will rise; paper bags — inflating and deflating them slowly is supposed to teach breath control; a large coin — clench it hard between your buttocks — it must not fall while you sing; a lighted candle — hold or place it so the flame is about ten inches in front of your mouth as you sing and the flame should remain bent, but it should not flicker or go out; a grand or upright piano — grab it under the treble end of the keyboard with the hand not holding the candle and try to lift it while you sing; two or three books — balance them on your head while singing — if they fall off, start the aria over; a glass of water — lie on your back on the floor and place the glass on your chest — now sing — if the glass doesn't fall off, you breathed correctly; if it does tip over, you'll need two more props — a mop and some dry clothes.

•

Oddly enough, each and every one of these offbeat props may have helped some singer rid himself of a bad habit and replace it with a new and, sometimes, a better one.

So, if you are anxious to improve your singing technique, you might try the piano-lifting exercise with one hand while balancing books on your head, clasping a silver dollar in your rear, pushing your shoulders down, plugging your nostrils with two small corks, and holding a lighted candle right in front of your face. Now sing your favorite aria and record the results on tape. After that immediately sing and record the aria again without props, lowered shoulders, candles, etc. Now find a German-trained recording engineer or acoustics man who would like to measure, analyze and graph out the various sounds you made with and without props. Only via such experiments can a performing artist benefit from the latest advances in science. [Hah! High level idiocy!]

Here are some other interesting tidbits of advice from voice teachers:

"Bigg-a mout' — bigg-a voice," quoth tenor/teacher Bernardo de Muro to his students. For "dee bigg-a mout'," make a mouth like a fish, don't pucker up like a hen's rear end. *"Bocca di pesce, non culo di gallina."*

To give you more oral space, have your tongue surgically shortened at the tip by a quarter of an inch or so. This *has* been tried. To produce head voice, think of stinking fish.

If you're not in good voice, coast, but even if you're in great voice, in ensembles, move your lips but don't sing. For big high notes, have some friend do them for you behind the scenes. That way you will never abuse your valuable vocal equipment.

If you are a prima donna, whisper to each of several male admirers that you will sing your love aria "just for you, my darling." Find out where each is sitting in the audience. Look soulfully in the direction of one of them for the first third of your aria. Then stare with love in your eyes at the second for awhile. Then aim your gazes at the third, etc. You can make a lot of male hearts flutter that way.

If you are a soprano or a tenor and have a big high note in your final aria, give it all you've got and hold it as long as you want. When the public leaves the theatre, that note is in any case all they'll remember of your singing.

Speed up in the easy places and slow down in the hard ones. It will all even out in the end, but if it doesn't and you have notes left over when the others are finished, *don't sing them*!

Similarly, for a recital, tell your pianist not to play any final bars after you've finished singing. They could interfere with your applause.

Also, for a concert, practice in front of a mirror turning pages in the score so you can do it with proper nonchalance and panache.

Remember, if you can fake sincerity, vocal security and musicianship, you'll have your listeners in the palm of your hand.

In opera or recitals smile triumphantly after each number no matter how badly you mangled it. If you botch a note or two badly, glare frigidly at your accompanist, the conductor or some colleague on stage.

If you sing sharp or flat, do so with poise and aplomb and make it seem part of your interpretation. In rehearsal if you lose your place in the music, always explain at great length why.

The good time to anger and upset your rivals is just before they go on or while they are performing. For example, in the big duet or trio numbers, just as your colleague launches into the most beautiful part of the music, do something to distract, such as hitching up your pants or dress. [I saw Richard Tucker do this on two occasions.]

Ah yes! Now we finally come to that extravaganza known as the Master Class where big name singers and former stars tell students, aspiring to become stars, how to get there. Some students wax quite enthusiastic about such half or one-day sessions because then they can say they studied with Horne, Callas, Tebaldi, Bergonzi or whoever.

Voice teachers at the Bolgona Consevatory roped retired tenor Galliano Masini into giving a Master Class where he was to listen to some dozen voices. Masini promised himself to criticize gently no matter how many unredeemable mediocrities turned up. He knew among any bunch of novice singers there would be plenty of "fireflies mistaken for lanterns."

"What are you going to sing for me, my lad?" Masini asked the first candidate.

"*Una furtiva lagrima*, Maestro."

"Bravo! Let's hear it."

When he finished, Masini commented, "Yes, you are indeed a lyric tenor. How long have you been taking lessons?"

"Two years, Maestro."

"Good! Continue to study. I'd like to hear you again in another two years. Who's next?"

"I'm going to sing *Vissi d'arte,* Commendatore."

"Very good. *Avanti. Coraggio!*"

When she had finished, she asked Masini what he thought about her career prospects.

"Well, Signorina, you're singing with your voice placed way back here," said Masini, tapping the back of his neck.

"What can I do to correct that, Maestro?"

"Well, I understand there's a top-flight professor of surgery here in Bologna. Perhaps he could move your mouth around to the rear of your neck."

Voice teacher to a new tenor student: "I have here in my shirt pocket the high-C for you".

"When you have paid me for enough lessons, I'll give it to you".

Student: Maestro, do you advocate pear-shaped tones?
Teacher: It depends.
Student: What do you mean?
Teacher: It depends which end of the pear you want to hear first.

•

"People who have heard me sing, say I don't."

—Mark Twain

•

No amount of personality projection makes up for vocal trouble.

—Sir Rudolf Bing

•

Madness seems to improve the art of singing.

—Albert Einstein

The story goes that in the 1920s a singer from Naples emigrated to New York and opened a small voice studio. For one dollar each he sold his students wine bottles of air from Naples, explaining, "Eena Naples–eh everybawdy has a beautifoola voice. Dee air eesa verry, verry gooedah fora dee voice. You breeda dis aireh you voice become-a *molto, molto bella*."

Teaching singing is a wide-open profession. Anyone can hang out a shingle. Conservatories, universities and schools naturally like to insist on some sort of academic degree or at least a more-than-paltry singing career. Despite fine organizations, such as the National Association of Teachers of Singing, and basic standards for accrediting teachers, the backstage stream of sarcastic stories about voice tutors flows on and on.

CHAPTER 19

IMPRESARIOS, GENERAL MANAGERS AND AGENCY IDIOTS

"OPERA THEATRES EXIST TO BE FILLED," muttered Verdi, but composers, musicians and singers know they cannot fill them without help. Why? Because they have neither the time nor the skills to deal with manic prima donnas, rent theatres in distant cities, haggle contracts, launch publicity, sell tickets, and, most important of all, line up the financing for an opera season. If opera people agree on anything, it is that a season will not succeed without an impresario with acute business sense, diplomatic aplomb — and lots of brass.

Until part-way into the 20th-century, anyone cockeyed enough to become an opera impresario also had to be a jack-of-many-trades, a Type-A personality with a psychiatrist's skills, with the mindset of a high-stakes gambler, the cunning of a lion tamer, the blarney of a roadshow barker, and the patience of a nursery school teacher. Moreover, to survive he had to sell lots of tickets and draw crowds. If he succeeded, he could become rich as the Ancient Greek Croesus. So the prospect of money, power and fame lured many paragons of hokum out of non-musical pursuits into opera. Even the circus world's "Prince of Humbug," Phineas Taylor Barnum of Barnum and Bailey Circus, took a stab at managing. He boasted he had grossed over $700,000.00 in cool, heavy 19th-century dollars, from just one American concert foray by "the Swedish Nightingale," soprano Jenny Lind. He pocketed about half a million of that gross.

Inside each impresario and general manager there lurks a frustrated performer whose deep passion for theatre life lets him put up with incredible crises, hellish imbroglios as well as the scorn and ingratitude of those who owe their jobs to him. Any average person would quickly throw in the towel, but then few average people are incurably addicted to "the smell of greasepaint and the roar of the crowd."

Like Barnum, most old-style impresarios were flamboyant, self-made men. For several hundred years, they ran the world of opera. It is impossible today with unions and boards of directors to imagine what tyrants they were. Composers, singers, and orchestra players were fully under their thumbs. *They* commissioned new operas. It was *they* who paid composers for exclusive rights to opera scores. It was *they* who leased and operated theatres, and lastly, it was *they* who hired and fired stars or anyone else, often on a mere whim.

Since these old-time "Mafia-crats" of opera wielded so much power and pocketed so much of the cash, backstage jokes most often skewer them as ludicrous, penny-pinching, despotic charlatans, or ham-headed nitwits — and more than a few were just that. Composers and opera folk in general have resented bitterly that ignorant impresarios, general managers, and singers' agents have prospered mightily without knowing much of anything about music.

One butt of many stories and much ridicule was Commendatore Pasquale di Costanzo, general manager of the San Carlo Opera in Naples. Di Costanzo owned a large upholstery business and was more of a fan than an expert.

One day, a San Carlo conductor told di Costanzo the orchestra had to have an English horn. "You know our money problems," protested di Costanzo, waving his arms in southern Italian distress. "Why can't you use an Italian horn, or a French horn? Why must it come from England?"

·

When a San Carlo board member recommended *Tristan and Isolde* for the following season, di Costanzo panicked, "No, no! That would cost too much! Maybe we could do *Tristan* next season and *Isolde* the year after."

·

When the San Carlo was considering Alban Berg's *Lulu*, a board member objected because Countess Geschwitz in the opera is a lesbian, but again di Costanzo was right there with a solution: instead of a lesbian, call her an Austrian.

·

Tony Corcione, mime at La Scala, despised di Costanzo. He would clench his teeth whenever he heard di Costanzo's name, and utter a strong wish to meet di Costanzo alone at night in some dark alley.

·

General Manager: "I need a good tenor for *Otello* right away."

Singers' Agent: "For a good tenor for *Otello* these days there's penury."

General Manager: "Send him over."

Singers' Agent: "Send who over?"

General Manager: "Penury."

•

A few singers manage to land contracts without an agent's help. For example, an imaginative Italian baritone with a flair for imitating voices used his talents on the phone to inveigle a contract from the Rome Opera. He simply had his girlfriend phone the main opera office, saying Prime Minister Mario Scelba was on the line and wished to speak with the general manager. When the general manager came on, our baritone, sounding exactly like Scelba, said, "My dear chap, why don't you give some work to that fine young baritone, So-and-so? I'm sending him over at *ten* tomorrow morning. I shall not forget your help in this matter." A contract awaited Signor X's signature the next morning.

•

An American baritone, who for the purposes of this story we shall call Oscar Meisler, says he too found phone calls quite effective. Through the operatic grapevine he learned that during rehearsals at a London theatre, the lead baritone for a difficult role had fallen ill. Since Meisler knew the role somewhat and was a quick study, he phoned that theatre saying he was a *New York Times* reporter sent by the New York office to find and interview "the celebrated American baritone Oscar Meisler." The theatre people said they'd never heard of any Oscar Meisler.

The following day he called again in a different voice saying that the Paris office of the *Herald Tribune* wished to send a reporter over to interview Oscar Meisler, the famous American baritone. Did any one know at which hotel Meisler was staying? Again the theatre folk said unfortunately they did not.

The same afternoon Meisler phoned that theatre in his normal voice and said, "This is Oscar Meisler. Are there any messages for me?" The theatre gave him his messages and suggested he drop by for an interview. When they discovered he "knew" the problem role, they gave him a contract. He lasted one performance.

•

Mario Lanza's career-launching ploy was classic: after learning where the world-famous conductor Serge Koussevitsky was staying, he booked a room in the same hotel right next door and sang up a storm. Koussy was so impressed by the voice he wanted Lanza then and there for the tenor part in Beethoven's *Ninth Symphony*, but, as Koussy's assistants soon discovered, Lanza couldn't read a note and was an obdurately unmusical learner. The voice, however, was door opener enough. Hollywood did the rest.

•

Impresarios know how to get a fast reading on any up-and-coming singer without any audition: just ask a couple of his or her rivals, "How well does So-and-so sing?" They realize appraisals by rivals might not exactly highlight a singer's strengths any more than the newspaper critiques a singer sends the impresarios will highlight defects. Beverly Sills told singers aspiring to join the New York City Opera, "Don't bother sending me your newspaper clippings — after all, you wouldn't send me any that weren't glowing and positive, now would you?"

•

After tenor Giancinto Prandelli lost two front teeth in an auto mishap, Liduino Bonardi of Milan, his manager, mournfully announced to Prandelli's friends and fans in Milan's Galleria that Prandelli was done for, finished. Without front teeth, how could he possibly sing? Bonardi by this time had had over 30 years experience handling singers. When it was explained to him that front teeth really don't have much to do with voice production, he squinted in scornful disbelief.

•

What then was Bonardi's musical background? Well, he started out as errand boy and doorman at one of the most important theatrical agencies in Milan, the agency of Giuseppe Lussardi. What did Bonardi do as doorman? He had visitors write their names on slips of paper that he would take into the inner sanctum and then come back and tell the visitors to wait. He also mailed letters for the agency, had passports visaed for artists leaving for abroad, etc. When Lussardi died, Bonardi inherited the agency.

•

Lussardi's and Bonardi's attitude toward singers can be summed up in two quotations. Lussardi often boasted, "I audition all singers who come to me. In a basket of rotten apples there will always be one or two that are edible." Bonardi privately confessed he had no earthly idea if a singer was good or bad, adding, "Singers for me are like cattle: how much can I sell them for?"

•

The tenor auditioning had just finished his last aria when the agent asked, "Who taught you voice?"

"Sir, I know it's hard to believe, but to tell the truth, no one taught me. I have never taken a lesson. I have a natural voice. What little I have learned, I learned from listening to old 78-speed recordings of such greats as Caruso, McCormack, Gigli, and Pertile."

"Aha! That," commented the agent, "would explain the scratchiness in your voice."

•

In Paris around the 1900s, the wealthy board members of the Théâtre de l'Opéra had been invited by the general manager to talk over the following year's program. Over coffee, a heated debate erupted about the cost of putting on Rossini's *Semiramide*. A foppish young millionaire listened with impatience to both sides of the argument. Finally be erupted. "Why all this fuss about a 'semi' Ramide, when for 20,000 francs more we could put on an entire Ramide?"

•

138

Successful impresarios have often sprung from odd backgrounds. The first impresario in North America arrived from England in the 18th century. His name was Thomas Lanier, an uncle of poet Sidney Lanier. He had left England in a great hurry for a very simple reason: after being arrested for selling paintings he had forged, he was offered a choice: going to jail or to America.

•

Italy around 1900 had many very colorful opera entrepreneurs. Perhaps the most notorious and colorful was Domenico Barbaja, who became an international superpower in opera thanks to money he had amassed from a chain of brothels and gambling casinos. Later, his casinos, for convenience and efficiency's sake, were set up inside his opera houses and the brothels next door.

•

Another very fascinating Italian impresario early in the last century was Ciro Ragazzini of Parma. He was a constipated baritone who never made a career. His true profession was one not usually associated with opera: he raised and auctioned hogs. Nevertheless, the opera troupes he assembled, including troupes to South America, often had better casts than La Scala itself. Old Ragazzini had an excellent ear and was a stickler for putting the right voice and the right actor in the right part, particularly in the minor roles.

He was also a notorious pinchpenny, often waiting to pay singers until they were about to hop on the train. He would then pay them off in small coins. Once the train had chugged away and they had counted all the change, they frequently discovered he had gypped each of them by five or ten lire.

•

Impresario: "Your son has a fine voice and I think I can include him in next month's concert."

Mother: "How nice! But what will be the honorarium? I mean, his fee?"

Impresario: "Dear Madam, I wouldn't think of accepting cash for his first appearance.

•

"A true impresario never pays anyone."
— Alfredo Salmaggi, Brooklyn impresario

•

"Good Lord! Those blank stares remind me I have to sing a concert tonight."

CHAPTER 20

ALL CRITICS HAVE ASSES' EARS

"Venom from a contented rattlesnake"
— Percy Hammond

IN THE 18TH CENTURY, *La Critique Musicale* in Paris printed a review calling Rossini's music "vulgar, tasteless and trivial." Rossini and his common-law second wife, soprano Olympe Pelissier, wanted to show proper appreciation. So they prepared two gifts: one for the critic and one for the editor of *La Critique Musicale*. Each parcel was beautifully wrapped and contained two large asses' ears, gently nestled in a bedding of horse manure. The Rossinis thoughtfully included their calling cards.

•

Composers and opera performers love critics the same way trees in Manhattan's Central Park love dogs, but unlike trees, composers and musicians, if they feel peed-on, can erupt in anger and fight back. Caruso once vented his spleen by scribbling "LIARS" on every review in the morning papers. Also in New York, tenor Giacomo Lauri-Volpi slugged a critic. In Italy of the the 1950s, a disgruntled mezzsoprano publicly bit one critic on the ear, and brained another with her *Trovatore* score. Another mezzo, Bulgarian Elena Nikolai at La Scala, slapped critic Franco Abbiati because he had written, "you couldn't understand a word she was singing."

•

In Vienna a well-known critic had just died in utter poverty. One of his few friends approached Richard Strauss to ask if he would like to join other musicians and contribute 50 kroner to help pay for the poor fellow's burial. Strauss replied, "Here's 100 kroner. Now you can bury two critics."

•

A critic whom Igor Stravinsky particularly disliked was Paul Lang of the *New York Herald Tribune*. Here is a snippet from a Stravinsky telegram to the *Herald Tribune* which that paper published: "The only blight on my eightieth birthday is the realization my age will probably keep me from celebrating the funeral of your senile music columnist."

•

According to Samuel Chotzinoff, Arturo Toscanini, when asked about a reviewer's remarks about his conducting, vesuviated; "Do notta talka to me abouta creetics! Dey know *NOthing!*"

•

Too bad Toscanini wasn't listening in the 1950s when the Italian State Radio announced "Verdi's *Requiem* directed by Maestro Arturo Toscanini." Between sections of the *Requiem* leading Italian music critics and musicologists commented and rhapsodized: "Who but Toscanini could have produced those trumpets?"; "Only Toscanini can bring out the full power and tension Verdi intended"; and so on and so forth.

At the end of the program it was announced, "For purely technical reasons, we were unable this evening to bring you the *Requiem* directed by Maestro Toscanini. You heard instead, the *Requiem* conducted by Maestro Vittorio de Sabata." The experts left by the side door.

•

Those Italian critics were not alone. Others have also made even more cockeyed verdicts. Here are a few critiques that have caused opera people either to yawn or smile — or both.

•

The *New York Times* critic, commenting on *Carmen*'s American premiere in 1878, judged the opera was "neither very good nor very original" was certainly in "bad taste."

•

English critic Henry Chorley wrote of his first *Traviata*. "Consumption for one who is to sing! A ballet with a lame sylphide would be as rational."

•

Italian critic Carlo Bersezio, after the world premiere of Puccini's *La Boheme*, wrote, "*La Boheme* has not made a deep impression on the listeners, nor will it leave much of a trace in the history of the opera stage. The composer would be wise to write it off as a passing error. Let him consider *La Boheme* an accidental mistake in his artistic career."

•

According to Jules Renard of France, "A critic is a soldier who shoots at his own troops." Another Frenchman, Tristan Bernard, disagrees and describes a critic as "a virgin who wants to teach Don Juan how to make love." Vladimir Pachmann added that critics are "the eunuchs of art; they talk about what they cannot do." So Sibelius was right when he wrote that "no monument was ever built to a critic."

Nevertheless, opera people grudgingly admit critics are useful. First of all, they keep theatre managements and performers more on their toes than they would be without critics. Second, they help some operagoers know what they ought to think or say about last night's performance. Third, their articles lure people to listen to unknown works by unknown composers, operas that almost no one would otherwise bother to hear. Critics and operagoers with ultra-conservative tastes would probably agree that Paul Valery's sour grapes about painting could also apply to opera: "Modern painting is made by writers. If they would just keep quiet, it would disappear within a year."

•

As mentioned, many critics are seized by verbal indigestion when they hear modern works. Here are a few quotes which appeal to opera folk.

On Ermanno Wolf-Ferrari's *The Jewels of the Madonna*: "Paste."

•

Paul Zschörlich, critic for the Berlin *Die Deutsche Zeitung* in Berlin, on Alban Berg's *Wozzeck*:
"As I came out of the Staatsoper last night, I did not feel as if I were coming out of a public art institution, but out of a lunatic asylum. On the stage, in the orchestra, in the hall, outright madmen!"

•

New York author and critic Samuel Chotzinoff on Berg's operas:
"It is my private opinion that Mr. Berg is just a bluff. But even if he isn't, it is impossible to deny that his music [?] is a soporific, by the side of which a telephone book is a strong cup of coffee."

•

Lawrence Gilman of the *New York Herald Tribune* on *Porgy and Bess*:
"Sure-fire rubbish!"

•

Gilman on Massenet:
"Jules Emile Frédéric Massenet, this intrepid composer, gifted with the spiritual distinction of a butler, the compassionate understanding of a telephone girl, and the expressive capacity of an amorous tomtit."

•

Henry Theophilus Finck on Strauss' *Elektra*:
"In *Elektra* Strauss lets loose an orchestral riot that suggests a murder scene in a Chinese theatre. If the reader who has not heard *Elektra* desires to witness something that looks as its orchestral score sounds, let him next summer poke a stick

into an ant hill and watch the black insects darting, angry and bewildered, biting and clawing in a thousand directions at once. It's amusing for ten minutes, but not for two hours."

•

Joseph Stalin's advice to Dmitri Shostakovich:
"Soviet composers should write music that workers can whistle on their way to work."

•

German author, philosopher and esthete Johann Wolfgang von Goethe on Mozart's *Magic Flute*:
"It requires more culture to understand the virtues of the *The Magic Flute* than to point out its defects."

•

Wagner's sometime-friend, philosopher Friedrich Nietzsche on *Parsifal*:
"Christianity arranged for Wagnerians."

•

What would Richard Wagner say if he knew that *The Ride of the Valkyries* and other loud samples of his wares were chasing pestiferous vagrants and panhandlers out of Metro stations in Montreal? Other measures to stop this segment of society from accosting subway passengers and demanding handouts hadn't worked, but opera music, particularly the Wagnerian kind, caused them to take flight. "'Hiya-ha-ho! It's outta the Metro we go!"

•

Friedrich Nietzsche on Jacques Offenbach and Wagner:
"Offenbach … is a most intellectual and high-spirited satyr … a real relief after the sentimental and at bottom degenerate musicians of German romanticism … Offenbach has even more right to the title of 'genius' than Wagner. Wagner is heavy and clumsy."

•

Wagner on Offenbach:
"Look at Offenbach. He can do what the divine Mozart did. … Offenbach could have been a Mozart."

•

Art critic John Ruskin on Beethoven:

"Beethoven always sounds to me like the upsetting of bags of nails with here and there an also-dropped hammer."

•

Baron von Kotzebue on the overture to *Fidelio*:

"All impartial people who know and love music were in perfect agreement: nothing has ever been written in music that is so disjointed, shrill, and offensive to the ear. The most piercing modulations occur in truly atrocious harmony, and the few petty ideas he has only complete the disagreeable and deafening effect."

•

The New York Sun's critic, William Henderson, on Shostakovich's *Lady Macbeth of Mzensk*:

"*Lady Macbeth of Mzensk* is a bed-chamber opera. We see much of the coarse embraces of the two sinners, mumbling and fumbling about in bed. Shostakovich is without doubt the foremost composer of pornographic music in the history of the art. The whole is little better than a glorification of the sort of stuff that filthy pencils write on lavatory walls."

Certainly, within the trade, the most snide critics of singers are other singers. Take Italian basso Enzo Feliciati as an example.

In 1951, Feliciati sang the part of Sparafucile in *Rigoletto* in many theatres throughout Italy. This outburst of *Rigolettos* marked the 100th anniversary of that opera and the 50th anniversary of Verdi's death. During one performance, the stage director was miffed to see Feliciati shuffle away as far as he could from the baritone during their first act duet. At intermission, the director asked, "Why on earth did you do that?"

"Well," Enzo responded, "that *Rigoletto* has such an ugly voice full of ugly notes, I was afraid my ears would be ruined. That's why I moved away from him."

Feliciati's sarcastic remarks eventually landed him among the unemployed. Other singers refused to appear with him. Finally, after leaning on his agent for months, the agent offered him the part of the King in an *Aida* to be staged in Brescia. There was one catch: Enzo must promise to speak no evil. He agreed.

A day after the last performance, Enzo was strolling among other singers in the Galleria in Milan, when someone asked, "How was that *Aida* in Brescia?" Feliciati remembered his oath of silence and replied, "I'm not going to say a thing." "But how was Callas?" Enzo pointed down with his thumb and made a face. "What about del Monaco?" inquired another. Feliciati lifted both arms in mock despair and rolled his eyes toward heaven. "How was the mezzo?" Feliciati waggled his hands in a "so-so" gesture. "And Pasero?" Feliciati spat on the ground. A model silent critic, who said all without uttering a word.

•

Do composers, singers and conductors read reviews? No, lots of them claim they don't. Sometimes, however, that merely means someone reads them for them. Typically, a spouse or a close chum sneaks out before breakfast, buys the day's papers and smuggles them back into the hotel. If the reviews are bad, perhaps they are only read aloud, so the artist can truthfully say he or she never saw them. If, on the other hand, the review is a nice one or skewers rival singers, the performer and entourage can gloat and quote all over town.

•

In Milan back in 1912 a catastrophic performance of the *Barber of Seville* was acidly reviewed by critic Romeo Carugati. "BARBER ASSASSINATED AT THE TEATRO VERDI" read the headline. Listed as his assassins were the names of the conductor, soprano, tenor, baritone, bass, even the chorus master.

Now, by sheer coincidence a new chief of police from Naples had just taken over in Milan two days before. Over his morning espresso his eyes bugged out as he read "BARBER ASSASSINATED AT TEATRO VERDI." Without reading further, he grabbed his uniform hat and shouted for two senior officers to come with him to investigate a murder. "Aha," he mused, "here's a good chance to show the people, the police, and crooks of Milan who's in charge."

Rushing into the cafe next to the theatre, the chief went up to an old timer, "Do you know anything about this murder?"

"Sure. It happened next door. You should arrest ALL of 'em," the old gent said, hardly glancing up from his newspaper.

"Who was the victim?"

"A Barber of Seville."

"A Spaniard, eh!" mused the chief.

At this point, officer Number Two whispered something to the chief who turned beet red. And Milan snickered for weeks.

Let's round off things with some critical bon mots:

"Aida drowned in the Nile."

•

"The soprano had a very high-pitched bust."

•

"She was a singer who had to take any note above A with her eyebrows." — Montague Glass

•

Ernest Newman's description of Nellie Melba's voice: "uninterestingly perfect and perfectly uninteresting."

•

[Jenny Lind] sang bad music the best. — Author unknown

•

"Fräulein X made her debut last night in *Walküre*. Why?"

•

"Miss Jones rendered Puccini."

•

"Thou singest like a bird called a swine." — John Ray

•

"She was a town and country soprano of the kind often used at funerals for augmenting grief." — George Ade

•

"The program was very balanced: half of it he sang very well and the other half very badly."

·

"Just before midnight the curtain closed and the opera with it."

·

"Madame Montserrat Caballé hung delicate chains of cadenzas from the ceiling of La Scala until finally she brought down the house."

·

"Half the audience whistled while the other half applauded those who were whistling."

·

"Thanks to her powers of execution, the audience hung on every note."

·

U.S. President Calvin Coolidge at a White House concert was asked what he thought of the soprano's execution. Cal replied, "I'm in favor of it."

·

In defense of critics, Lawrence Gilman wrote that the opera profession "either views you as a ruthless destroyer or useful builder of reputations … your praise of artists will be regarded as their due, and your dispraise as the natural result of ignorance, animus, dyspepsia, or all three."

CHAPTER 21

OPERA DOLLARS AND CENTS — MOSTLY NONSENSE

TICKETHOLDERS AT THE ACADEMY in Philadelphia were squirming and checking their watches. Why hadn't *Aida* begun? It should have started ten minutes ago. Suddenly, impresario Alfredo Salmaggi stepped to the footlights and announced, "*Aida* is-a cancel, because-a zee tenor ees-a een-deespoz-ed." At that, the tenor in question, Bernardo de Muro, burst through the curtains behind Salmaggi and shouted in Italian, "I'm not indisposed! This bastard won't pay me." They then disappeared between the curtains amid shouting and arm waving. Minutes later de Muro had his cash and the opera got under way.

Not all theatres keep their promises to singers: "If you sub for us tonight, we will give you a lead role in *Tales of Hoffmann* next season." Unfortunately, performers often discover Sam Goldwyn was probably right: "An oral promise isn't worth the paper it's printed on." Moreover, even if you take your contract with you, you might have to create quite a scene to get everything the contract guarantees you.

Speaking of *Aida*, back in the 1930s, tenor Galliano Masini received a cabled offer of 5,000 lire to do *Aida* at the Arena in

Verona. He wired back: "5000 OKAY FOR ACTS ONE AND TWO STOP. FOR ACTS THREE AND FOUR LET'S NEGOTIATE STOP. MASINI."

•

During a rehearsal in Paris, the prima donna made a very dramatic lurch and broke her necklace. Pearls cascaded, bounced and skittered all over the set. The rehearsal stopped as singers costumed as dukes and duchesses stooped around, rumps in air, picking the baubles up.

While waiting, the conductor commented wryly to the soprano, "Well, you must have bought those large pearls with the high fees they pay you in Dallas, Chicago and Buenos Aires."

"No, Maestro," the diva replied. "They're imitation pearls, and I could barely afford them with what they pay me here in Paris."

•

Asked about the money side of his long career, a German tenor said, "In the good years it was wine, women, and song, and in the bad years mama, beer, and gramophone."

•

In Canada a senior citizen insisted he should pay only half-price for his ticket. Why? He was stone deaf in one ear and so he'd only be able to hear half as much as other ticket holders.

•

Employers often use a rather shopworn gambit to turn down singers' requests for a raise, but it's a gambit that can boomerang. Here are two classic examples:

Diva Adelina Patti asked P.T. Barnum for her usual sky-high fee of $5,000.00 He replied that not even the President of the United States made that much. "All right," replied Patti, "have the President to sing for you." P. T. caved in and Adelina got her five grand.

Giuseppe di Stefano at the Met hit up Rudolf Bing for a big raise. Bing said that only Kirsten Flagstad pulls down that high a fee.

"Then let Flagstad sing my roles."

•

An 18th-century impresario, Andrea del Po owed 2,000 ducats at the end of the Naples opera season to the soprano Anna Strada. She was at the time the ugliest female treading the boards. In fact, London nicknamed her "The Pig." His solution? Instead of paying her — he married her.

•

Managers of important houses, such as La Scala and the Met, have often gotten away with paying rock-bottom fees to singers debuting in their theatres, because they know singers can cash in on the prestige of having sung there.

In 1962 American heldentenor Jess Thomas finally received a call to come back from Europe and sing his debut at the Metropolitan. As a splendid Wagnerian tenor with a rare voice, he was already world famous. So when Rudolf Bing offered him a rather measly fee, he wrote to Rudolf Bing he felt entitled to at least the same amount as Del Monaco received when he made his Met debut.

Bing replied that the Met archives from 1950 were luckily still intact. Since Del Monaco was paid $250.00 [allegedly] per performance, Bing would be delighted to offer Jess that amount — since it was far less than Bing's original offer.

•

Mariano Stabile at La Scala was assiduously taught the part of Falstaff by Arturo Toscanini and Stabile's score was filled with copious notes in Toscanini's hand. After Stabile had become the most celebrated Falstaff of his generation, he approached Toscanini and said he deserved a raise. Toscanini turned on him and snarled, "If you insist on more money, I'll take the first baritone I find off the street and teach him to sing Falstaff better than you do." The subject was dropped.

•

Parsimonious Francesco Tamagno (1850-1905) was unquestionably the foremost Italian dramatic tenor from 1874 until 1898, when heart trouble began to slow him down. Verdi chose him for many important roles. He had a clarion, ear-splitting voice that could almost crack security glass. He was in high demand for dramatic tenor roles in major theatres throughout Europe and the Americas.

So, Tamagno soon became quite well-to-do, but since he had grown up as one of 15 children of a poor Torino innkeeper, he had very thrifty habits. Parting with even a few lire was for him a harrowing experience.

While starring at the Met, a hotel chambermaid caught him washing his own socks and underwear. She also noted that he stayed in his room and supped on bread, cheese, and salami, if no one invited him to dine out. On the few occasions, such as his daughter's wedding dinner, when he had to pay, he would doggie-bag leftovers and have the waiters collect any wine from half-empty bottles or glasses and send it over to his home.

On an Atlantic crossing, the general manager of the Met, Maurice Grau, learned that this star tenor had sold his first class ticket, pocketed the money, and was now traveling in steerage.

In Milan at Verdi's hotel Tamagno often joined Verdi, Boïto and friends in low-stakes card games. Verdi begged Boïto and the others, "For the love of God, let Tamagno win at least a few lire. If he's losing at the end of the evening, he'll be angry and sulk for a week."

Tamagno lived alone and very thriftily in Varese the last period of his life, while the locals grumbled about his miserly ways. When he died, his daughter inherited his fortune, but her husband gambled it away in less than two years.

CHAPTER 22

OPERA DOLLARS AND CENTS — MOSTLY NONSENSE

OPERA FOLK STRONGLY SUSPECT CONDUCTORS prefer orchestral works where they are the highest star with the highest fee. In opera, conductors have to smile and be jovial while sharing the limelight and curtain calls with "mere singers," who disrupt and sabotage their performance in many ways: ignoring the conductor's tempi and baton, holding their high notes forever, and worst of all, provoking wild ovations.

"Watch me! Watch me! Follow my tempi," the stick waver orders, knowing full well singers prefer conductors who watch and follow them. Conductors also know the big-name artist on stage will cop the highest fee and will usually prevail in any head-on confrontation. After Toscanini, few conductors have pulled down a higher fee than the star soprano or tenor.

Why is an important singer paid more than an equally important conductor? General manager Maurice Grau at the old Met had the obvious answer, "No one will pay a nickel to stare at a man's back."

•

Conductor-versus-singer battles are legion and rehearsals are the best stage arenas for displays of one-upmanship, spite, and prestige arm wrestling. After all, at rehearsals the contestants play for an elite audience — orchestra, chorus, singers, stagehands, *et al.* — a jury well equipped to judge who won and who lost — and to spread the glad tidings.

•

The locale is Rome in the hot, humid summer of 1960. Jussi Bjoerling, tenor, and Sir Georg Solti, conductor, are rehearsing *Un ballo in maschera*:

Solti: Mr. Bjoerling, I wonder if we could repeat the aria and if you would be so kind as to sing it a bit faster.

Bjoerling: Maestro, for over 20 years I have always sung *E scherzo o è follia*? the same way in the major theatres of the world. My public would not understand why I change tempo *now*.

Solti: Nevertheless, Mr. Bjoerling, I would be very grateful if, for this particular recording, you would use the slightly different tempo I suggest.

Bjoerling: Maestro Solti, do you think people will buy the records because I'm singing or because *you* are conducting?

Solti: Mr. Bjoerling, London Decca has placed me in artistic charge of this recording so I must request that you follow my suggestions.

Bjoerling: In that case, Maestro, may I suggest you and Decca find another tenor. I'm going back to my hotel. (Exit Bjoerling)

Bjoerling died on September 9, 1960, less than three months after this incident. But for this stubborn duel, *Un ballo in maschera* would have been his last complete opera recording. To win the skirmish, the conductor lost the war. [Incidentally, parts of this account that were doing the rounds in Scandinavia may be apocryphal, according to Bjoerling's esteemed biographer, Andrew Farkas. Nevertheless, no member of the Bjoerling family was present during the final set-to with Solti. Moreover, in New York in rehearsal Bjoerling had once asked conductor, Fausto Cleva whether he thought people would buy tickets because Cleva was conducting or because he, Bjoerling, was singing.]

•

Scene: Dress rehearsal of Franchetti's *Siberia* at the Lirico Theatre in Milano, diminutive Maestro Leopoldo Mugnone on the podium, and sturdy baritone Titta Ruffo on stage.

Mugnone: Ruffo, why the devil are you standing there like a fencepost?

Ruffo: [menacingly] Mugnone, we'll settle accounts later out in the alley.

Mugnone: [quaking] My son, act the part any way you please!

•

Conductor Tullio Serafin: I must say, Ettore, you have a fabulous memory!

Baritone Ettore Nava: Oh, thank you, Maestro!

Tullio Serafin: Yes ... you're making exactly the same mistakes you made 15 years ago!

•

Basso Tancredi Pasero had heard all about Toscanini's habit of spewing insults at new singers. So, in 1917 when he first came on stage at La Scala for rehearsals of *Don Carlo*, he was primed to talk back.

Toscanini first sarcastically asked, "And you, where'd you drop in from?" Then Toscanini wondered out loud why a strapping young fellow like Pasero was not in a military uniform and fighting for his country.

"I didn't just drop in from anywhere, Maestro. For three years I've had your contract at home, but I never wanted to accept it simply because YOU were here. I don't need this work. I've plenty of offers elsewhere, and, frankly, it's far more enjoyable to sing with people who smile and don't insult others and call people names."

"That's enough!" said Toscanini and the rehearsal got down to business. Eventually, Pasero and Toscanini had a fairly good working relationship, even though they often disagreed about this or that interpretative or musical detail.

•

At a dress rehearsal for *Pagliacci* the baritone singing Tonio had a run-of-the-mill voice. For the difficult phrase "*al pari di voi*" in the Prologue, he took a deep breath, but between "di" and "voi" he let out a loud fart, panicking all within earshot. The conductor commented, "In some ways, that was the best sound you've made all week."

•

After rehearsing the Sextette from *Lucia* over and over again for two hours, the conductor finally threw up his hands and shouted, "I've taught you all I know — and you know NOTHING!"

•

Tenor Anton Schott was singing so far off pitch during the dress rehearsal of *Lohengrin* that the conductor announced, "He's a Swine-knight, but no Swan-knight."

•

Soprano Mary Garden was wearing a very revealing costume, so the elderly conductor reproached her. "Miss Garden, if I were in your place, I would put on more clothing."

Amid chuckles from the orchestra, Mary shot back, "I'm quite ready to believe what you say, Maestro."

Baritone Karl Kienlechner was enraged. The conductor had sabotaged him during a Bayreuth performance. At the final curtain in full view of the audience, Kienlechner slugged the conductor, and knocked him off his feet. Not a very smart move: Kienlechner was banned for life from all German stages.

•

Chaliapin singing at London's Drury Lane in 1913 was having one of his usual knock-down-drag-out arguments with the conductor. Finally, Chaliapin yelled at him, "Your head is a toilet."

A year later, there was Chaliapin back at Drury Lane in another opera, but with that same conductor. This time the Russian basso was so pleased with the conductor, he gave him a big bear hug and kissed him, Russian-fashion, on both cheeks. At that a cast member chortled, "Look, Chaliapin is kissing the toilet."

For centuries, orchestra conductors were mere drill sergeants with very, very narrow authority. It took Wagner and the Germans to magnify them into aristocrats and high priests. Even so, until well into the 20th-century in many lands playbills and even aria record labels did not bother to mention the conductor's name.

Wagner was fussy, sarcastic, demanding, and ambivalent about conductors. Although he and other Germans elevated their importance and let them become titans of the podium, he sneered at one point that all a conductor had to do was keep time and have a bit of personality. [According to others, a conductor should speak loudly and carry a little stick — otherwise he's a mere semi-conductor.]

Orchestra members love to test the emotional stability and patience of conductors and they have found ways to bamboozle and sabotage any they dislike.

Once during his term as artistic director of Hammerstein's Manhattan Opera, the orchestra tested Cleofonte Campanini's acumen by playing down half a tone. Campanini, as they expected, noticed nothing.

•

At Torre del Lago, Argeo Quadri was conducting a rehearsal. He declared the timpanist was incompetent and summarily insisted on a replacement. Since there was no replacement available, the theatre manager simply had the sacked timpanist put on other clothes, a moustache, a wig and some makeup. Quadri noticed nothing.

•

The kindest, after-performance comment singers make about conductors is often, "Well, he did better tonight."

•

Bruno Martinotti in the 1980s was conducting a rehearsal in Torino. Right in the middle someone in an orchestra seat tossed a ten lira coin at him, perhaps to indicate what they thought he was worth. Ten lire was worth less than one American penny.

•

The chorus conductor for *Die Meistersinger* was delivering a long, irate tirade aimed at the sopranos when a tenor piped up, "Maestro, does that apply to the tenors too?"
"Yes, but an octave lower."

•

An English conductor gave a tongue lashing at rehearsal to a bass viol player who turned up drunk. The next evening this conductor mounted the podium to conduct *Traviata* only to find the pages of his score glued together. Nothing to do but conduct the prelude and Act One from memory.

•

At La Scala in the very early 1990s, a performance of *Traviata* was being videotaped before a live audience. In the middle of the second act, a loud alarm clock went off. A search revealed it had been placed right under conductor Riccardo

Muti's chair under the podium. Several instrumentalists were suspected of trying to get revenge for some real or imagined slight.

•

Anarchical displays by Italian orchestra members are not rare. In Bologna, a principal wind instrument player oinked like a pig whenever he disapproved of a conductor — a rather strong insult in Italy.

•

A violinist named Horowitz had played in the Met orchestra for over 20 years when his nephew asked, "Unc, which are your favorite operas?" "The shortest ones," was the terse reply.

•

In rehearsal at La Scala the American timpanist dozed off. Conductor Riccardo Muti stopped everything, had someone wake him up, and with barely concealed anger said that this was the first time in his whole career anything like this had ever happened. The timpanist caused gales of laughter when he replied with a yawn, "For me it's the second time: it also happened to me with Böhm."

•

Conductor to soprano, "Miss Blatz, would you mind giving the orchestra your A so they can tune to it."

•

Tenor: "Maestro, did ya hear that high-C I hit in the aria?"
De Fabritis: "Yes, I heard it. What a shame the orchestra was playing sharp."

•

During rehearsal with the Cincinnati Symphony Orchestra, soloist Eileen Farrell watched as the conductor went through his get-in-the-mood ritual: first, he stood with eyes closed, head bowed, for almost 20 seconds as if seeking divine guidance. Then, as he slowly raised his baton, Eileen let out a loud, long, resonant belch.

•

Famous Italian conductors Gianandrea Gavazzeni and Olivero de Fabritis were strolling one afternoon in Gavazzeni's home town of Bergamo. Pausing silently in front of Donizetti's home, they read the bronze plaque on the front wall. "I wonder what they will write on our houses," Gavazzeni mused aloud.

De Fabritis replied, "FOR RENT."

At his hotel in New York, Sir Thomas Beecham accepted an unexpected person-to-person call from Dallas, Texas. The enthusiastic voice greeted him in a thick Texas drawl, "Mistah Beecham, aah am not only a majuh benefactah of grayund op'ra, but aah am also the presidint of the English Speakin' Union of Day-llas, Texas."

Beecham interrupted, "I cahn't believe you," and hung up.

Beecham once confided to the American stage director Rexford Harrower, "Händel's music would sound better orchestrated by Berlioz."

A quite bestial conductor-to-cast encounter involved an oft-described dress rehearsal of *Aida* led by Beecham.

Act One had gone badly. Beecham used his sourest wit to excoriate the singers and taunt them to do better in Act Two. In vain! It was even worse. The high point of absurdity occurred during the Triumphal Scene when a small Indian elephant splattered pachyderm droppings on the stage. Beecham stopped the rehearsal and commented tersely, "As an actor the beast leaves much to be desired, but what a *superb* critic!"

Serge Koussevitsky introduced several Russian operas to Western Europe when he worked in Paris, but by the time he sailed to America he apparently had lost all taste for opera. One day at the stage door of Boston's Symphony Hall, someone yelled at him, "Koussevitsky, you're God." Koussy stared at him awhile and finally replied, "I know my responsibility."

•

On another occasion, a stage-door admirer said, "Koussevitsky, you're the greatest conductor in the world!"

He protested, "No, no. There are other good conductors." Then turning to his wife said, "Natasha, who are they?"

•

It is said that Koussevitsky once recommended to the trustees of the Boston Symphony that a monument be erected to him at Tanglewood in recognition of his contributions to music in America.

In Italy when opera buffs reminisce about conductors, three stiletto-tongued Maestros invariably come up: Arturo Toscanini, Leopoldo Mugnone, and Antonio Guarnieri. We may never see their like again because their sarcasm would today be considered intolerable abuse.

Let's start with the most fascinating conductor of the last century, fiery Arturo Toscanini, that devout anti-dilettante with his unique and disturbing combination of mature musical genius, Po Valley macho morality, egotism, petulance, patriotism, humility, generosity, honesty, showmanship, guile, and childlike simplicity. Rivals such as Thomas Beecham could dismiss him as that "Italian bandmaster," while others, such as Richard Strauss and Giacomo Puccini, hailed him as the greatest conductor of all. As Strauss put it, "there are many Cardinals, but Arturo Toscanini is the Pope."

Toscanini, for his part, had little if anything good to say about other conductors. Gustav Mahler was "A crazy nut." Leopold Stokowski was simply "That clown!" Karl Muck was "the Beckmesser of conductors." Furtwängler was "a gifted amateur" and Koussevitsky "a Russian boor." In return, Furtwängler fired back, "I begin where Toscanini leaves off" and Koussevitsky declared Toscanini was "an Italian peasant." Once at La Scala, seated in a box, Toscanini and family heard an opera conducted by Mario Rossi. Watching Rossi, Toscanini became so agitated and made so many deprecating gestures and faces, his embarrassed family had him move to the rear of the box where he couldn't be seen.

•

Geraldine Farrar, the lovely, charismatic soprano, had several rehearsal spats with Toscanini at the old Met. The first time she exclaimed, "But, Maestro, I am the star here." He replied, "I'll keep your secret." When she said the same thing at another rehearsal, he said, "The only stars I know are in the heavens." As a footnote to that exchange, in Toscanini's home town of Parma they say not only had Toscanini used the "stars-in-the-sky" gambit long before he met Farrar, but so had other conductors. A snappy retort is worth using more than once.

•

Toscanini's friends loved to ask his reactions to this person or that event because he had quotable opinions on just about everything. Once at the end of a modern music congress in Venice, a friend heard him mutter, "Thank God, it's over; now let's fumigate the theatre."

•

Toscanini made another pronouncement when asked about modern music: "Music is not like wine. It does not improve with age. It is either good or it is bad."

•

Over the centuries conductors have found none-too-subtle ways to stop singers from holding their high notes too long. At La Scala in rehearsal Caruso held a high note too long. So,

Toscanini put his stick down, crossed his arms over his chest, and said, "Let me know, Caruso, when you've finished."

•

Baritone Antonio Laffi, as the 'Nightwatchman', also held high notes too long in a rehearsal of *Meistersinger* at La Scala. Toscanini stopped the music and said, "Who is this peanut gallery baritone?"

•

In 1943 during the Second World War, at his home in Riverdale, New York, Toscanini fumed over the brutal war, bogged down halfway up the peninsula of his beloved Italy. Much of Italy's suffering he blamed on the stupidity of American politicians and the Pentagon. Asked by Professor Gaetano Salvemini of Harvard for his opinion of Franklin Delano Roosevelt, Toscanini blurted out, "He's a tenor." In this case "tenor" is Italian shorthand for self-centered, vain, and, above all, stupid.

•

Also during the Second World War Toscanini heard that basso Ezio Pinza had just spent several hours in jail, after allegedly making some pro-Mussolini remarks in a Boston bar. The very anti-fascist Maestro sighed, and, pointing to his throat, said, "If singers have any brains, they are here."

•

Once, pointing to an ample-busted soprano's throat, he said, "If you had up there what you have down there," pointing to her chest, "what a singer you would be!"

•

Conductor Dick Marzolo, born in London, sometimes stood in for the elderly Arturo Toscanini at rehearsals in New York.

One day during their usual post-rehearsal get-togethers, Marzolo reported that soprano Licia Albanese's husband had hauled off and cuffed his wife hard, right in front of everybody because she had made a musical mistake. Marzolo added, "Wasn't that despicable?"

"Absolutely," replied Toscanini, "He should have taken her home first."

•

At a party in his home, Toscanini, in a confidential mood, told his attractive, blond neighbor, Maritza Bolaffio, "You know, the orchestra members think I am terrible. I shout at them and break batons, but I'm not angry. If I didn't do these things, they wouldn't listen to me. — But, for the love of God, don't let them know!"

Conductor Walter Ducloux once asked Toscanini in Lucerne what experience he would like to relive if he could turn back the clock. Toscanini replied that he would like to relive an evening when he was 16 and playing cello at the Parma Conservatory. Ducloux, somewhat surprised, asked why. The Maestro replied, "That was the evening I decided to become a conductor."

Toscanini confessed to a friend, "I kissed my first girl and smoked my first cigarette the same day, and ever since I've never had time for tobacco."

A prime rival of Toscanini in Italy was little Leopoldo Mugnone from Naples. Mugnone often conducted perched on a chair. Mounting the podium at La Scala where Toscanini had conducted the night before, Mugnone took out his handkerchief, flicked it over the seat of the chair, held his nose, and made a clear allusion to Toscanini's hometown of Parma: "It stinks here of parmesan."

By all accounts in Italy, Mugnone was not only a great conductor, but also a very quick-witted quipster. Of the dozens of stories about him, here are a couple:

Alfredo Salmaggi, the colorful impresario in Brooklyn, brought Mugnone to New York for the 1920–21 season to conduct *Aida* and *La Gioconda*. He was supposed to conduct *Rigoletto* as well, but after ferocious newspaper critiques, he decided to cut his losses and hightail it back to Italy.

Adolfo Mariani of Asti's restaurant drove with him from his hotel to the dock to board a liner bound for Naples. On the way, Mugnone insisted the cab stop at Columbus Circle, where he got out, walked over to the statue of Columbus, shook his fist, and swore mighty Neapolitan oaths ending up with, "your mother and all your sisters were whores ... curses on you for ever discovering this damned country." Then he got back in the taxi and calmly proceeded to his ship.

•

Mugnone also had his favorites and to them he showed his kindlier side. One Mugnone protégé was an elderly cellist in the San Carlo Opera orchestra named Pasquale. Poor Pasquale now and then embroidered the music with flights of notes never imagined by the composer. Why didn't Mugnone fire this undisciplined hacker? Well, Pasquale had six mouths to feed at home. One day during rehearsal when Pasquale was sawing away out on cloud nine, Mugnone stopped the orchestra and said in the Neapolitan dialect, *"Pasqua'!! Pasqualí, prend' 'a cinquina, ma non sunnà."* [Pasquale, Pasqualino, go ahead and collect your pay every Friday, but don't play.]

Antonio Guarnieri (1881–1958) was a highly respected conductor, an anti-dilettante, a perfectionist, famous for bringing out splendid sonorities in the operas he conducted. Furthermore, he was a great Italian Wagner specialist. Unfortunately, outside Italy, neighboring countries and Argentina, he was a virtual unknown, partly because he disliked "canned music" and avoided making records. He did leave behind a diamond mine of anecdotes filled with fast repartee and some of the most frigid putdowns this side of the North Pole.

One day in Milan, a fellow musician asked Guarnieri, "Maestro, by any chance do you know the telephone number for La Scala?"

"Yes. It's zero-zero-zero-zero."

"No. Seriously, I must call the general manager."

"Add another zero."

•

Modernistic opera composer Alfredo Casella (1883–1947) once announced to Guarnieri, "Maestro, do you realize I was born the same year Wagner died?"

Guarnieri in a bored voice replied, "Tragedies of such dimensions seldom come alone."

One day Guarnieri received an unexpected invitation to Benito Mussolini's office. Once there Mussolini took out his Stradivarius and asked Guarnieri to hear him play. When Il Duce finished fiddling, he turned to Guarnieri and said, "What do you say, Maestro?"

"Inside his own home, every one plays as best he can," was Guarnieri's reply. [The same story is told of Serafin.]

•

After Wagner's son Siegfried had conducted a Wagnerian work at La Scala, Guarnieri told him, "Your father's works are so great not even you can ruin them."

•

Antonio Guarnieri was a thorough-going perfectionist. During a rehearsal he fired point-blank an elderly cellist. That cellist was his father.

On another occasion he asked a careless string player to go out in the auditorium and listen to the orchestra. This done, Guarnieri inquired, "Well, Giuseppe, what did you think of our sonority?"

"It is magnificent, perfect, Maestro!"

"You see, Giuseppe, we sound much better without you."

•

An important doctor of medicine in Siena believed he had a fine tenor voice and pestered Guarnieri both directly and via friends to audition him. Guarnieri was rehearsing with the orchestra Donizetti's *L'Elisir d'amore* and agreed to let the doctor sing *Una furtiva lagrima*. As he had fully expected, the physician didn't have a voice for opera. Guarnieri stopped him after the first two phrases of the aria and suggested he move two steps to the left and start the aria again. Again after the first two phrases he stopped him and told him to move still further to the left. After this happened for the fourth time, the doctor said, "But, Maestro, if I move again I'll be behind the curtain."

"That's where you belong," was Guarnieri's reply.

●

Hungarian conductor Andras Korodi confessed to a former high school chum, "I dreamt a few days ago I was conducting *Lohengrin* and I woke up and discovered I was."

●

Soprano: "Oh Maestro, I've taken that score to bed with me every night".

Sir Thomas Beecham: "Well, soon we shall have the immaculate conception".

CHAPTER 23

POOR, POOR COMPROMISED COMPOSERS!

FOR ALL OF OPERA HISTORY, most composers have come up short on fame and even shorter on fortune. Publishers, impresarios, musicians and singers, on the other hand, have raked in plenty, cashing in on the composer's works.

For centuries, opera authors had to be attached to some court or powerful aristocrat. Otherwise, as musicians they had no steady income. They received only a pittance plus room and board. Their dawn-to-dusk court duties often included composing works for a social event that evening, giving music lessons, playing the church organ, directing the choir, conducting orchestras, producing and directing concerts and operas, and so on. Most people thought of them as mere scratchers of little balloons on paper. In many courts they wore lackey uniforms and ranked in the social pecking order just above cooks.

Moreover, opera composers had little or no control over how and where their operas were performed. Impresarios and publishers owned all rights to their operas and without copyright protection, any "opera-tunist" could and did cop their best tunes. Opera authors must have felt like parents of babies who were whisked away for adoption at birth.

Adding insult to injury, a superstar's fee for singing one performance and the impresario's cut of the night's gate often topped the composer's entire earnings for the opera. Singers and publishers also have been paid royalties on their recordings, but composers reaped no such benefit. Puccini called this "musical piracy."

As if that were not enough, for several centuries star singers customarily mangled the composer's music with their own cuts, additions, frills and trills — and composers could do nothing about it. Then, in the latter part of the 19th century, star conductors gained the upper hand and forced singers to stick closer to the score, but very few composers had any control over how conductors butchered, cut up, sliced, and served up their music.

In recent decades, stage directors and designers have replaced conductors and singers as the worst deformers of composers' intentions. And who will take over when their era ends?

Puccini described himself as "a mighty hunter of wild fowl, beautiful women, and good libretti." He could have added fast cars and motorboats. In New York he struck a great bargain with a wealthy fan: in exchange for a handwritten, signed and dedicated copy of *Musetta's Waltz*, the New Yorker bought for Puccini a very fancy, state-of-the-art motor launch, which was then shipped to the Italian lake near Puccini's home.

The two little vignettes about Pietro Mascagni and *Cavalleria Rusticana* show how powerless composers have been. Singers, conductors, and stage directors agree it is wiser for a composer not to come to rehearsals and to give singers, conductors, etc., any advice they have before rehearsals begin.

For that same world premiere, Mascagni lost a loud, knock-down-drag-out argument with the famous tenor doing Turiddu, Roberto Stagno. Stagno had completely misinterpreted the meaning of one line in the libretto and Mascagni tried to set him straight. Stagno blew up and said in an insulting tone, "I am Roberto Stagno and I'll interpret the part any way I please." Ah, tenors!

A famous rehearsal spat occurred during *Cavalleria* rehearsals for a Naples performance that Mascagni conducted himself at the Arenaccia. Before rehearsal, Mascagni had told tenor Galliano Masini to give his voice the widest possible vibrato and choke with emotion saying the last words of farewell to his mother at the close of the opera. "When you say '*Mamma, addio*' hold on to the word Mamma and shake your arms and voice in desperation."

Masini did as he was told, but Mascagni's irrepressible wife Lina, famous for putting in her own two cents, was sitting in the front row just behind her husband. She jumped to her feet and shouted at Masini, "No! No! We can't put up with cheap ham acting like that."

Mascagni spun around in fury and threw his baton at Lina, and shouted, "Damn it all, I TOLD him to do it that way."

Masini came to the footlights and said, "Make up your minds what you want. He says do it this way, and she says do it that way."

Aside from arm wrestling with performers and musicians, composers must save some energy for fighting among themselves. Historically, when an opera composer says something nice about a colleague, it's most often about a dead one. Wagner without question has been the most popular target for other composers' darts and slurs, with Giacomo (Jacques) Meyerbeer coming in a distant second. Some claim that more has been written about Richard Wagner than about any other person except Jesus Christ and Napoleon Bonaparte.

Let's look at some of the mud pies and ripe tomatoes composers have flung at each other. Giacomo Meyerbeer is our first target.

Wagner after hearing Meyerbeer's *L'Africaine*:
"Effects without a cause."

Rossini on the music in Meyerbeer's *Les Huguenots*:
"Music? I didn't notice any."

Robert Schumann on Meyerbeer's *Le Prophète*:
"Last evening I heard Meyerbeer's *Le Prophète†*"
[With the sign of the cross, Schumann indicated it was "dead on arrival."]

Debussy on Wagner:
"Wagner was a glorious sunset mistaken for a rosy dawn."
[This was also philosopher Oswald Spengler's opinion.]

Bizet on Wagner:
"*Rienzi* ...an undescribable racket, a jumble of Italian motives, a bizarre and bad style ...music of decadence rather than the future. Wretched numbers! Admirable numbers! ... Some claimed, 'It's bad Verdi!' Others said, 'It's good Wagner!' ...'It's sublime! It's frightful! It's mediocre!'"

Wagner on Gounod:
"An inflamed artist, always in a swoon [who wrote] that theatrical parody of our German *Faust* ...the music is all surface sentimentality."

Wagner on Verdi:
"Swine!"

Wagner on Italian composers:

"An orchestra in the hands of an Italian composer is nothing other than a monstrous guitar which he uses to accompany arias."

Gounod on César Franck [whose operas were all failures]:
"The affirmation of incompetence pushed to dogmatic lengths."

Tchaikovsky on Modest Mussorgsky's *Boris Godunov*:
"From the bottom of my heart I consign it to the devil. It is a most insipid and low parody of music."

Stravinsky on Richard Strauss:
"I would like to admit all Strauss operas to whichever purgatory punishes triumphant banality. Their musical substance is cheap and poor."

Stravinsky on Dmitri Kabalevsky:
"A horror!"

Stravinsky on Aram Katchaturian:
"Not even a horror!"

Schumann on Gaetano Donizetti's *La Favorite*:
"I heard only two acts. Puppet theatre music!"

Antonio Salieri upon hearing of Mozart's death:

"Had this man lived, the rest of us would not have been able to earn even a crust of bread with our operas."

•

Giovanni Paisiello on German composers:
"The Germans were mainly bad singers and therefore concentrated primarily on the study of harmony rules to achieve their musical effects; whereas Italians, being singers by nature, had no need of harmony — their melody could express anything."

•

Rossini on German composers:
"Rules are for the mediocre ... They usually begin with instrumental music which may make it difficult for them later on to subject themselves to the restrictions imposed by vocal music. It is hard for them to become simple."

•

When Franz Schubert showed Carl Maria von Weber the scores of some of his first attempts at opera, Weber opined that, "First operas, like first puppies, should all be drowned."

•

Richard Strauss' father on his son's *Salome*: "It sounds like nothing but ants crawling up your trouser legs."

•

At the request of a humdrum colleague, Boïto examined a song said to be composed by Giuseppe Mercadante.
"This music is simply too awful to be by Mercadante."
"Well, Maestro, what would you say if I admitted I wrote it?"
"I don't believe that either; it's far too good to be yours."

Has any opera composer authored more keen-witted quips, quibbles and stories than Gioacchino Rossini? Most definitely not. No other had his waggish gift for bon mots, aphorisms, puns and putdowns. Indeed, it is impossible in France and Italy to chat about opera tomfoolery without a Rossini story cropping up. Opera composers are a pretty serious, dour lot. What a delight it is to run across a great composer who is both jolly and able to laugh not just at others, but at himself. Here is a miniature sampling of Rossiniana:

A private collector in Italy owns two likenesses of Rossini glued side-by-side on heavy paper. In the left one he is standing at about the age of 25. The other is a famous photo of him as a short, fat old geezer of almost 70 seated in a chair. Beneath these portraits Rossini penned the words, *"Figaro su ...Figaro giù,"* [Figaro up ... Figaro down.] [signed] Gioacchino Rossini.

•

When admirers told Rossini on his 70th birthday that they had collected 20,000 francs for the erection of a Rossini monument in Paris, he said, "What a waste! Give me the cash and I'll stand on the pedestal myself." [Actually, since Rossini was born on February 29th in a Leap Year, this was not his 70th birthday but only his 19th.]

•

A Parisian lady of high station brought her daughter to sing for Rossini, and said in preface, "Maestro, if you believe my daughter sings well, I should like her to have a career; if not, I would prefer her to stay an honest woman."

Rossini listened to her very run-of-the-mill warbling, "Your daughter could sing if she had a voice; it's better she should be an honest woman, if she's able."

•

"Händel's name doesn't need an *umlaut*, but Gluck's does." For those of us whose German skills are a bit rusty, Händel without the umlaut is "Handel," meaning "commerce or business," implying that Händel wrote commercial music and was a good businessman. Since Glück means "luck," Rossini is saying in a backhanded way that, considering his music, Gluck had a lot of luck.

•

175

A pot-bellied, would-be baritone asked if Rossini thought he could have a stage career. Rossini answered, "As a singer certainly not, but perhaps as a dancer."

"But, Maestro, don't you see I'm fat?"

"Well, I've seen bears dance."

•

For most of his adult life, Rossini wore a hairpiece to hide his baldness. One day he said, "There are those who say this is not my hair. I paid a lot for it. If it isn't mine, whose is it?"

•

Rossini did note, however, that cuts have one advantage for the composer: "Anything cut is not booed."

•

A young composer asked Rossini to do him the honor of looking over two of his songs and tell him which one he ought to have published. Rossini glanced rapidly over the first one and handed both back, saying, "I'd print the second one. It couldn't possibly be worse than the first."

•

In another instance, a composer for piano brought two short pieces and asked Rossini to listen to them and say which one he liked best. The young man had no sooner played the final chord of the first when Rossini said, "Never mind playing the second. I like it better already."

•

After looking over the manuscript of a new composer's work, Rossini handed it back to him saying, "There's much that's beautiful and much that's new in these pages."

"Oh, thank you, Maestro. That's saying a lot."

"Yes, but what you have that's beautiful is not new — and what is new is not beautiful."

It is well established that Richard Wagner suffered from chronic constipation, but so far scholars and musicologists have not bothered to assess to what degree, if any, this malady influenced his music — or, the other way around — to what extent his music may have influenced his constipation.

•

Conductor Luigi Arditi (1822–1903) tells in his memoirs of an evening when he was playing the score of *Tannhäuser*. Next door his daughter inquired, "Who's playing the piano, mama?"

"Your father, dear."

"Oh, I thought it was the piano tuner."

•

"I dozed off [in Vienna] during *Tannhäuser*, but then, many of the Germans around me were also snoring."

— Giuseppe Verdi

•

"*Tannhäuser* is not merely polyphonous, but polycacophonous."

— *Musical World* (1855)

•

"...the devil's uproar music of this bullheaded fellow, fed full with brass and sawdust, who, by his destructively insane egotism, by mephistophelian, mephitic and most poisonous hellish miasma blown up into Beelzebub's Court Composer and General Director of Hell's Music — Wagner!"

— *Musical Herald* (1884)

•

"...Wagnerian din ... inspired by a riot of cats scampering in the dark about an ironmonger's shop."

— Alexandre Dumas

•

"The music of Wagner imposes mental tortures that only algebra has the right to inflict."

— Paul de Saint-Victor

•

"There's more music in *La donna è mobile* than in all of *Tristan und Isolde*."

— Igor Stravinsky

Apollo could charm all the animals with music, but all Wagner could do was make one "low hen grin."

•

A friend once pointed out to Wagner that if Lohengrin was indeed the son of Parsifal, Parsifal must have forgotten his vow of chastity. Coldly, Wagner replied, "Chastity can work miracles."

•

Brockway and Weinstein in their book *The World of Opera* also took a heavy sideswipe at *Parsifal*: "*Parsifal* is silly. ... How could anyone, even Wagner, make credible music drama out of this sanctimonious, neurotic, completely undigested twaddle?"

•

Parsifal was also hardly a favorite of King Ludwig II of Bavaria. When he saw his first and only performance, he left after the first act, muttering, "Not even ten wild horses could drag me back in there."

•

"*Parsifal* is an opera that begins at five-thirty. Three hours later you look at your watch, and it's only twenty to six."

— George Jean Nathan

•

"Formlessness elevated to a principle."

— Eduard Hanslick

•

"*Siegfried* was simply awful. It would put a cat out of its misery and would turn boulders into scrambled eggs. ... All this crap could be reduced to 100 measures, because it's always the same thing and always equally tiresome."

— Richard Strauss

•

When Sir Thomas Beecham was asked whether he liked Wagner less now than he used to, he replied, "That is impossible."

Wagner, knowing many people passionately disliked him, composed the following little birthday poem for himself:

Im wunderschönen Monat Mai
Kroch Richard Wagner aus dem Ei.
Ihm wünschen, die zumeist ihn lieben,
Er wäre besser drin geblieben.

In the wondrous fair month of May
Richard Wagner crept out of his egg.
Those who love him most wish
He had done better and stayed in it.

•

In the late 19th century, a Viennese opera orchestra rehearsed *Tristan and Isolde* 75 times, at which point they told the conductor bluntly that the music was unplayable.

In the 1880s a wealthy businessman in Frankfurt found a great way to show his appreciation of Wagner. He had an exquisite bust of Wagner carved out of a rare African wood. He put the bust in his living room — with a hangman's noose around its neck.

•

Speaking of Wagner busts, Auguste Renoir painted a very telling portrait of him, though he was no admirer of Wagner's music. After a Bayreuth performance, Renoir was overheard to say, "No one has the right to be that boring."

CHAPTER 24

OPERA AND POLITICS

IN 1929 PAUL HINDEMITH'S SATIRICAL OPERA *Neues vom Tage* [Novelties of the Day] opened in Berlin and not long thereafter a series of performances began in Breslau. Among other things, the heroine of the opera praised flipping a switch and heating water by electricity instead of stinky, finicky, dangerous gas. The City Gasworks of Breslau was highly upset by this indirect attack on their business. They used all the political leverage they could muster and forced the authorities to ban all further performances.

•

Back in 1871, *Lohengrin* was slated to be the first Wagnerian opera to be performed in Italy. Where? At the Teatro Comunale in Bologna. An exciting prospect particularly for the area's opera buffs and the city government!

According to an oft told and embellished story, the mayor decided to invite Wagner himself to come to the first performance and sit with the mayor in the centre box. "This would be a great feather in my political cap," the mayor mused.

A flowery invitation was prepared and delivered by courier to Wagner in Venice and some days later the mayor had a letter with Wagner's reply which was ceremoniously slit open by the mayor with members of the town council as onlookers. But oh! What a nasty surprise: the answer was in German and no one in the room could read it. The deputy mayor suddenly remembered his secretary had studied German. She was called in and the mayor tersely told her: "All we need to know is this: is he coming or isn't he? Read it fast and tell us."

Scanning the two pages, she said, "He's very honored and pleased. His German is longwinded, but he ends up saying he will come". General applause around the table! Explosions of enthusiasm in the press, tickets for the first night rise to stratospheric prices on the black market, the head of the box office is fired for ticket finagling.

A couple of nights later, the mayor turns and tosses in bed. "How do I know that secretary is competent in German? What if he said he's not coming? I'd be a laughing stock and lose the next election!" A crony of the mayor had lived and worked in Germany, so he was asked on the sly to study the text carefully. His comments were: "He goes on and on about how honored he is, but he regrets that because of other commitments he cannot come."

Almost in tears, the mayor decides he must triple-check before cancelling any preparations. He knocks on the door of the professor of German at Bologna University and that worthy comes up with a still different version: "Wagner is honored, he has conflicting commitments, but he'll fix it so he can come anyway." The mayor smiled all the way home.

After all the brouhaha and preparations, Wagner never did show up.

The mayor's enemies found out that he'd never had a real word-for-word translation made of the composer's letter. What that letter really said and what actually happened is lost in the mists of time. The mayor was trounced in the next election.

•

Following its brutal invasion of Abyssinia in the mid-1930s, Italy's reputation plummeted in free fall and the League of Nations slapped on humiliating economic sanctions. In hopes of rescuing Fascist Italy's name from further disgrace, a rather hairbrained Director in the Ministry of the Press and Propaganda named Luigi Freddi penned the following confidential memorandum to Benito Mussolini:

"Is it at all possible that one could think today of putting on *Rigoletto*, that ferocious tale about a petty provincial tyrant who uses and abuses his subjects, a satrap who gets his jollies from kidnappings and murders? .... Is it at all possible in a

181

Catholic Italy that one could revive for the edification of the masses a drama such as *Tosca*, gloomy and grisly, soaked in blood, garnished with police abuses and judicial errors? ......Is it at all possible in an Italy that seeks to draw a moral line between the white and colored races, to put on *Aida* which dramatically exalts, I believe [for I never really understood the plot], the marriage of a white man with a negress whose father, but for the support of the League of Nations, could stride forth as the Negus, Emperor of Abyssinia?"

The man who wrote this profound nonsense had been a Fascist goon squad leader, the kind that force fed glasses of castor oil to any anti Fascist who dared to express his opinion. To reward his zeal, he was appointed to a cushy directorship in Rome. [Unfortunately, the Fascist government was quite racist, pilots boasted about aerial bombing of unarmed crowds of blacks in Africa, the Fascist secret police tortured war prisoners, including Americans, and Mussolini allowed Jews to be handed over to the Germans for extermination. An untypical, anti-historical and ugly page in modern Italian history!]

•

Backstage in many major theatres, the Singers' Union and particularly the boss of that union have much political power in deciding who sings and who doesn't. I recall Cornell MacNeil, because of his power at the Met, was nicknamed "Big Mac" Naturally, those singers who feel slighted often accuse the union bosses of favoritism and using criteria having nothing to do with music. In some countries the unions lobby to keep the number of foreigners gaining contracts as low as possible. In Italy it is also well known that each of the larger political parties and some ministers in the government now then succeed in pushing on stage their protégés.

CHAPTER 25

FINAL ODDMENTS, IRONIES AND AWARDS

THE EQUIVOCAL LEGITIMACY OF OPERA

OPERA WAS MISBEGOTTEN, MISCONCEIVED and born by accident around 1600 when some upper class gentlemen in Florence tried to find out how the ancient Greeks used music in their dramas. A noble endeavor, but, like Christopher Columbus, these fellows knew very little about where they were going or how to get there. Also like the great Genoese explorer, they discovered not what they set out to find, but something else new and great — OPERA.

Opera and America have changed dramatically in the four to five hundred years since their discovery. So wouldn't it be fun to see and hear how those aristocratic Florentines and Columbus would react to today's opera and today's America? You can bet, mixed in with their oh's and ah's, there would be torrents of good old-fashioned Italian Renaissance profanity.

OPERA IN ENGLISH — OR IN THE ORIGINAL LANGUAGE?

"Opera in English is silly. Nobody takes it seriously."
— Maria Callas

"What difference does it make which language they sing in: either way, you can't understand the words."
— Mrs. Jess Walters

"Opera in English, in the main, is just as sensible as baseball in Italian."
— H. L. Mencken

"Isolda was an Irish queen who always sang in German. Though why she canned her native tongue. I never could determine."   —N. Levy

"Opera in English? All right. But what English are you talking about? Recently, I had to memorize the 18th different translation of Bartolo's aria in *The Marriage of Figaro*."
— Italo Tajo, bass

Translations of 19th-century operas inevitably lose the antique flavor and lilt of the original. Worse still, Victorian translations, such as Edward Dent's *Don Giovanni*, stay as far as possible away from lechery and might well pass as bedtime stories for novices in a nunnery.

Learning both foreign languages and good diction is beyond some singers. Fyodor Chaliapin and baritone John Charles Thomas come to mind. There was a strong Russian tinge in every language Chaliapin used, whereas Thomas had an omnipresent American twang and "er" signature in all languages. American singers with southern accents so thick you cut them with a knife have a particularly hard time. One southern lass at Yale called the old Schumann ditty "Du beast wie eine Bloomer."

"Bloomer" instead of "Blume" also panicked the New York Chorus of Bridesmaids in *Lohengrin* when German conductor Karl Muck reprimanded them in rehearsal for raising their bouquets to their noses at the wrong time. He announced, "De ladies are zniffing zer bloomers too zoon."

A TYPICAL COVENT GARDEN REHEARSAL

I am Georgetta Psaros, mezzo soprano. I'll never forget the *Traviata* rehearsal in 1967. I sang Annina, the maid, to

Mirella Freni's Violetta. For the last act. the director, Luchino Visconti showed his talent for revitalizing with dramatic detail old 19th century opera stagings. For example, he told me to pick up Mirella Freni, carry her over to the bed and help put on her slippers. When I asked him how I should carry her, he said "Lift me." I tried, but couldn't. So, Visconti promptly swept me up and carried me across the stage. While this was going on, we enjoyed watching Robert Merrill, who, having nothing better to do, practiced golf strokes with Papa Germont's cane. Ah, the good old days at Covent Garden!

SNEERS, JEERS AND CATTY COMMENTS

"I sometimes wonder which would be nicer — an opera without an interval, or an interval without an opera."
—Ernest Newman, opera critic

"If you want a tenor on stage to look as if he's thinking, have him walk down a flight of stairs."
—Frank Corsaro, stage director

Asked what type of person can become a prima donna, Canada's wonderful opera comedienne Anna Russell replied, "a glorious voiced, sexy, independently wealthy, politically motivated, back stabbing bitch."

"Which do star singers relish most: glowing compliments about themselves, or scathing comments about their rivals? Answer: it's a toss up.'
—Anonymous

A FEW EPOCH-MAKING PERFORMANCES

You may be glad or you may be sad you missed these performances: The world premiere in 1961 in Zürich of *Porgy and Bess* in German. — The Tokyo premiere on March 24, 1935 of

Carmen in Japanese. — Or what about *Emperor Jones* in Dutch in Amsterdam? — Or the world premiere (1861) in Vienna of *The Tales of Hoffmann* when the theatre burned down, killing many in the audience. — The single performance in 1667 of Marcantonio Cesti's *The Golden Apple* with 67 scenes, 23 changes of scenery and, counting musicians, a cast of 1,000. — The performance at Covent Garden on July 12, 1833 of *Norma* "compressed into one act." — The all-female cast put together by soprano Luisa Tetrazzini for a *Barber of Seville* in San Francisco.

CANDIDATES FOR GREAT ACHIEVEMENT GOLD MEDALS

Energetic architect and sculptor Giovanni Bernini (1598–1680) is best known for his Piazza Navona Fountains in Rome and his colonnade and baldacchino in the Vatican. He also deserves a gold medal for opera: after all, he designed and built his own theatre, wrote the music and libretto for his own opera, produced it, did the stage design, painted the scenery, directed it, and sang in it.

If Bernini deserves an award, then Richard Wagner certainly rates a gold medal, for he did all that Bernini did, though he didn't paint the scenery or — thank God! — sing. Wagner is, moreover, the only major composer to organize his own theatre and all that went with it right down to the minutest details. For example, he concocted a sign with instructions for the men's room at his Bayreuth Festspielhaus, requesting men button up before leaving the room.

Marcella Sembrich (1858–1936) was a virtuoso soprano, pianist, and violinist. She performed all three genres not only in concert, but also in a performance of *The Barber of Seville* at the Metropolitan. At the Met she sang many years with equal acclaim in Italian, French, and German opera.

If an operatic sextathalon existed, Luigi Lablache (1794–1858) would probably win the gold medal. First, let's list the composers who wrote roles and songs for him: Verdi, Donizetti, Balfe, Beethoven, Bellini, Pacini, Mercadante, and Schubert. Second, his versatility as an actor saw him acclaimed as the best comic and dramatic basso of his century. Third, he wrote a famous method and treatise on singing. Fourth, he was the singing teacher of Queen Victoria of England, Tsar Alexander I of Russia, and Ferdinand I of Portugal. Fifth, his effective range spanned two octaves plus five falsetto notes. Sixth, his very flexible voice was so enormous and had such focus and power, he could, and occasionally did, blank out all other singers in the ensemble scenes. If medals were awarded for bulk and size of body, he would also be a contender for the gold: he stood about six feet four or five and in his prime weighed over 330 pounds. His sense of humor was also gigantic. As Leporello in *Don Giovanni*, he sometimes showed off by picking up Masetto and carrying him off stage under one arm. What a shame that such a phenomenal artist lived before recording came along and so remains "a sculptor who worked in snow."

Baritone Mariano Stabile is surely a gold medalist. His stage career ran from 1909 until 1965. That seems to be the longest uninterrupted opera career of any major male singer in modern times. On the distaff side Adelina Patti's stage career, stretching from 1859 to 1914, would be hard to beat. So, medals to Stabile and Patti for longevity both of voice and of crowd appeal.

Arturo Toscanini certainly rates a gold medal for achievements both as conductor and artistic director. Aside from his genius as a charismatic orchestra director, his feats of memory are unequaled. He conducted from memory 117 operas by 53 composers. In the non-operatic field he conducted without a score nearly 500 works by 175 different composers. We must also credit him with several innovations, things we take for granted today. He abolished the old custom at La Scala of leaving auditorium lights on during the performance. He was also the first to insist that late arrivers wait to be seated until after the first act — and he did away with encores.

The city fathers of Venice, the famous Council of Ten, deserve a gold medal too. In 1700 the Council issued an ordinance making illegal the old habit of spitting and tossing garbage or slops from the boxes and balconies down into the standees area, what we now call the orchestra seat area. Before that, the pit was truly the pits.

Sir Rudolf Bing deserves a gold medal as the first general manager at the Met who consistently tested people out in their parts before casting them.

NOMINATIONS FOR THE ALBATROSS PRIZE

There are also some contenders for booby prizes and membership in the "Opera Hall of Shame." — Beethoven's cook, who lit fires using sheets of his music manuscripts. — Bach's gardener, who used sheets of Bach's music to wrap the trunks of young trees. — Countess de' Micheli of Florence, who bought Caruso's Villa Bellosguardo at Signa in the 1920s and burned up lots of Caruso memorabilia on the grounds that Caruso's letters, etc. were private matters and should remain private. — The son of prolific opera composer Rinaldo di Capua, who sold a pile of dad's manuscripts as wastepaper. — Soprano Giulia Grisi, whose farewell concert and stage performances began in 1849 and lasted until 1866.

A FEW OBSCURE PROFESSIONAL PITFALLS

Here are several contretemps;
The Ambassador of my country gave a reception in my honor and botched my name when introducing me. [President

Gerald Ford would sympathize with this: he once introduced Beverly Sills as "Miss Stills,"] Had spoonerisms' Dr. Spooner introduced her, she would have been "Silvery Bells."

•

I was cajoled, harassed and embarrassed into singing a couple of *South Pacific* ballads at a party. An imposing matron sailed up to me and said, "You have a beautiful voice. You ought to do something with it." I thanked her and said, "Some people have even urged me to try the opera stage."

"Well," she rejoined, "that might be reaching a little too high, but for folk ballads and Andrew Lloyd Webber type of things, I think you'd do very creditably."

Later the hostess urged her guests to hear me on the coming Saturday afternoon broadcast from the Met as Gilda in *Rigoletto*.

I watched the matron's jaw drop. She bustled to the bathroom and re-emerged after I had left.

•

You arrive at the theatre only to discover your costume, mementos and other belongings have been anonymously moved to a smaller dressing room — or someone has cut your costume to ribbons.

•

I am a mezzo-soprano from Poland Springs, Maine, yet the President of the Ladies Thursday Morning Music Club announced that I was from Poland.

•

I am a New Yorker born and bred and a Verdi tenor with an Italian name. Two gushing ladies came up to me in Atlanta, Georgia. After they had oohed and aahed, one asked me what part of Italy I was from. When I told them I was American and from the Bronx, their smiles curdled and they walked brusquely away. [Until you become a celebrity in America, it's better to be a foreigner because you get more respect.]

THE OLD FIRE HORSE SYNDROME

At age 76, a celebrated early 19th-century Italian tenor, Domenico Donzelli, was honored by his hometown of Bergamo, Italy with a gala performance of *Rigoletto*. He had excelled as the Duke until his retirement many years before, but now, poor Donzelli was so crippled with arthritis that he could barely stagger about on two canes.

On the eve of the gala, it took several friends almost an hour to push his aching, complaining carcass into the Duke's costume, and another ten minutes for him to hobble, huffing and puffing, from his dressing room to a chair in the wings.

Cast and stage crew took bets the audience would howl with laughter as soon as this old codger started singing about his great prowess with the ladies.

As the Duke's entrance approached, old Donzelli slowly straightened up, stretched, handed his canes to a friend and then shuffled tentatively onto the stage.

Greeted by thunderous applause and yells from his old fans, he smiled, quickened his pace, and forgetting all aches and pains, he fairly bounded about, pinching every wench, and doing a very convincing facsimile of a young libertine.

Offstage, however, he had to be led doubled over with pain to a chair. All night long Donzelli felt no pain at all each time he heard that marvelous, rejuvenating applause.

OPERA HUMOR GOLDMINES

Like it or not, Italy was the birthplace, kindergarten and prime producer of opera, opera singers and good opera humor. Perhaps because life there is really more operatic. Some Latin and Slavic opera centres, and a couple of melting-pots such as Vienna and New York, are also goldmines of opera jokes; however where opera is taken awfully seriously — usually due to pervasive Germanic influence — an opera joke is not a laughing matter.

Bravo! You've managed to finish your stroll through this operatic funhouse. As you have seen, opera folk are just like other people — only a bit more so, as we predicted.

For the final curtain, we see a prima donna and tenor exuding bonhomie and mutual esteem:

Once the curtain shuts, however....

Fyodor Dostoevsky predicted over 150 years ago, "Beauty will save the world." While awaiting that happy day, let's relax and enjoy some mirth and music.

And now a final word from Oscar Wilde:

"Humanity takes itself too seriously. It is the world's original sin. If the caveman had known how to laugh, history would have been different."

— Oscar Wilde

***

Index

About the Author

STEPHEN TANNER shuffles between Southern California and Northern Vermont. He escaped his native Cambridge, Massachusetts to the Putney School, Middlebury, and Yale. After teaching at Yale and the Yale Music School, he escaped again into the American Foreign Service. His posts included Munich, Helsinki, Brussels and Milan.

This volume includes a few apt excerpts from his second opera book, *Quotable Opera — Aria Ready for a Laugh?* which was also published by Sound And Vision in 2003. His new award winning book, *Tours de Farce — Travel Travesties*, is a gather-all of tourist bloopers and is available signed and inscribed by the author via sntann@aol.com. At various times, he has thrown energy into studying nine languages, teaching Italian and German, singing, acting, playwriting, coaching singers in diction, lecturing on opera humor and foreign affairs, organizing concerts and variety shows for charity, fund-raising, tennis, figure skating — he was U.S. Junior Pairs Champion in 1940 — and in palling around with other musicians, theatre and opera people.

About the Illustrator

UMBERTO TÀCCOLA, a Tuscan, arrived in Montreal in 1967 and became a Canadian citizen, he is responsible for an outpouring of original artistic and literary works, as a self-taught painter, book illustrator, journalist, caricaturist, sculptor, poet and guiding spirit behind French and Italian language programs for Radio Canada as well as for TV and the theatre. American Vice President Nelson Rockefeller commisioned Tàccola to do a painting. Tàccola returned in 1980 to Isernia, a mountain town in his native Italy. There he has won important local and regional fine-arts competitions and awards, including in a public competition to select a medallion design to commemorate the millennium.

ACKNOWLEDGEMENTS

AMONG FRIENDS AND ACQUAINTANCES who have contributed to my accumulation, I want especially to mention and thank the following: Amy Albani, Alberto Angeli, members of the Appassionati Verdiani Clubs of Parma, Maestro Juri Aronowitsch, Gemma Bosini, Maestro Luigi Campolieti, Gina Cigna, Maestro Charles Conti, Maestro Flaminio Contini, Tony Corcione, Bice Adami Corradetti, Chandler Cowles, Bernardo de Muro, Dina de Muro Dieli, John Doms, Mario del Monaco, Claudio Desderi, John Dizikes, Douglas Doty, Maestro Walter Ducloux, Quaintance Eaton, Andrew Farkas, Hedwig Fichtmüller, Lorenzo Ghiglia, Giorgio Giorgetti, John Gualiani, Rexford Harrower, Olga Isacescu, Frederick Jagel, Joneva Kaylen, Maestro Karl Kienlechner, Antonio Laffi, Adolfo Mariani, Lorenzo Mariani, Giovanni Martinelli, Sergio Masini, Maestro Arturo Merlini, Luigi Ottolini, Dimitri Nabokov, Dr. Giuseppe Negri, Uriel Nespoli, Kari Nurmela, Leone Paci, Tancredi Pasero, Diane Perry, Nino Piccaluga, Henry Pleasants, Lynne Strow Piccolo, Giacinto Prandelli, Georgetta Psaros, Hildegard Ranczak, Maestro Aldo Reggioli, Maestro Francesco Riggio, Guerrando Rigiri, Maestro Luciano Rosada, Titta Ruffo, Maestro Mario Salerno, Maestro Kenneth Schermerhorn, Maestro Albert Schmidt, Rudolf "Sartore" Schneider, Joseph Scuro, Beverly Sills, Musa Silver, Paolo Silveri, Mariano Stabile, Martti Talvela, Luba Tcheresky, Barry Tucker, Richard Tucker, Maestro Robert Wallenberg, Emma Walters, Thomas Wellman, Gail White, and Maestro Orville White.

The overwhelming majority of materials in this compilation were told to me by those mentioned above.

The story about Beverly Sills in *Die Fledermaus* is printed with her permission. Five of the *Yells from the Balcony* appeared originally in the *Gazzetta di Parma* in Italy, which has given permission to reprint them. Several drawings are modified copies taken from *Schiller's Werke*, printed by J.G.Fischer in Stuttgart, in 1877. The item about Luigi Freddi's memo to Mussolini appeared in program notes of the *Teatro Comunale* in Florence.

The Toscanini; funeral wreath story in *Chapter 3* is also described in greater detail in Samuel Chotzinoff's biography: *Toscanini: An Intimate Portrait* published by Alfred Knopf in 1956.

For their artistic work, I would like to thank Umberto Tàccola and Mike Rooth for embellishing Umberto's fine cover illustration. I am most grateful to my incredibly patient wife, Nancy, as well as to Jeannine Young, Ann Staffeld, Amy Albani, Janet Pumphrey, Howard Banning, Peter Ringland, Leila Phillip, Anne Biller and my friends in Canada, Bruce Surtees, John Loweth, Lionel Kofler, David Barber, Mike Walsh, Jacky Savage, and my very helpful publisher, Geoffrey Savage.

Stephen Tanner
June 2005, Vermont

www.soundandvision.com

This printing June 2005
1 3 5 7 9 11 13 15 - printings - 14 12 10 8 6 4 2

Canadian Cataloguing in Publication Data
Tanner, Stephen.B
Opera antics & anecdotes
ISBN 0-920151-40-X
1. Opera — Humor. 2. Opera — Anecdotes
I. Title. II. Title: Opera antics & anecdotes
ML65.T36 1999   782.1'0207   C99-931899-3

Typeset in ITC Century Book
Printed and bound in Canada by Metrolitho, PQ

The Sound And Vision catalogue:

A Musician's Dictionary
by David W. Barber & Dave Donald
preface by Yehudi Menuhin
isbn 0-920151-21-3

Bach, Beethoven and the Boys
Music History as It Ought to Be Taught
by David W. Barber & Dave Donald
preface by Anthony Burgess
isbn 0-920151-10-8

When the Fat Lady Sings
Opera History as It Ought to Be Taught
by David W. Barber & Dave Donald
preface by Maureen Forrester
foreword by Anna Russell
isbn 0-920151-34-5

If It Ain't Baroque
More Music History as
It Ought to Be Taught
by David W. Barber & Dave Donald
isbn 0-920151-15-9

I Wanna Be Sedated
Pop Music in the Seventies
by Phil Dellio & Scott Woods
Caricatures by Dave Prothero
preface by Chuck Eddy
isbn 0-920151-16-7

Getting a Handel on Messiah
by David W. Barber & Dave Donald
preface by Trevor Pinnock
isbn 0-920151-17-5

Love Lives of the Great Composers
From Gesualdo to Wagner
by Basil Howitt
isbn 0-920151-18-3

Tenors, Tantrums and Trills
An Opera Dictionary from Aida to Zzzz
by David W. Barber & Dave Donald
isbn 0-920151-19-1

How to Stay Awake
During Anybody's Second Movement
by David E. Walden, cartoons by Mike Duncan
preface by Charlie Farquharson
isbn 0-920151-20-5

A Working Musician's Joke Book
by Daniel G. Theaker
Cartoons by Mike Freen
isbn 0-920151-23-X

Better Than It Sounds
A Dictionary of Humorous
Musical Quotations
isbn 0-920151-22-1
compiled & Edited by
David W. Barber

The Composers
A Hystery of Music
by Kevin Reeves
preface by Daniel Taylor
isbn 0-920151-29-9

How To Listen To Modern Music
Without Earplugs
by David E. Walden
cartoons by Mike Duncan
foreword by Bramwell Tovey
isbn 0-920151-31-0

Tutus, Tights and Tiptoes
Ballet History as It Ought to Be Taught
by David W. Barber & Dave Donald
preface by Karen Kain
isbn 0-920151-30-2

1812 And All That
A Concise History of Music from
30.000 B.C to the Millennium
by Lawrence Leonard
cartoons by Emma Bebbington
isbn 0-920151-33-7

The Thing I've Played With the Most
Professor Anthon E. Darling Discusses
His Favourite Instrument
by David E. Walden
cartoons by Mike Duncan
foreword by Mabel May Squinnge, B.O.
isbn 0-920151-35-3

More Love Lives of the Great Composers
by Basil Howitt
isbn 0-920151-36-1

The Music Lover's Quotation Book
isbn 0-920151-37-X
Compiled & Edited by
David W. Barber

Grabbing Operas by Their Tales
Liberating the Libretti
by Charles E. Lake
Illustrations by Mike Rooth
isbn 0-920151-38-8

Drone On!
The High History of Celtic Music
by Winnie Czulinski
isbn 0-920151-39-6

Quotable Pop
Fifty Decades of Blah Blah Blah
Compiled & Edited by Phil Dellio & Scott Woods
Caricatures by Mike Rooth
isbn 0-920151-50-7

Quotable Jazz
Compiled & Edited by Marshall Bowden
Caricatures by Mike Rooth
isbn 0-920151-55-8

Quotable Opera
Compiled & Edited by Steve & Nancy Tanner
Caricatures by Umberto Tàccola
isbn 0-920151-54-X

*

Quotable War Or Peace
Compiled & Edited by Geoff Savage
Caricatures by Mike Rooth
preface by Bruce Surtees
isbn 0-920151-57-4

Note from the Publisher

I would like to thank Steve Tanner for a great book. It never cesses to amaze me the vitality of this American Octogenarian.

This new edition now with an idex, will give knowledge and pleasure to lover's of music and opera provided one has a sense of humour.

If you have any comments about this book or any other title we publish, or if you would like a catalogue, please contact me at: www.soundandvision.com. I would really like to hear from you.
Our search continues for original books to publish. If you have an idea or book outline please contact us at our address: www. soundandvision com.

Thank you for purchasing or borrowing this book.

Geoffrey Savage

* * *